"Motherhood is one of the mc___ it can also be very isolating. D___ do motherhood with your peop___ ___ide that will help you find those teamma___ ___ the exciting mission of mothering."

Jennie Allen, *New York Times* bestselling author of *Get Out of Your Head* and founder and visionary of IF:Gathering

"Heather MacFadyen is the mom friend you've been looking for your entire life. She's not going to make you feel like you're behind or like you're messing it up—but she's also not going to try to pacify your fears, desires, or vision for your family. She's a kind leader, an amazing writer, and a faithful friend. This book is a gift from God to us, and I cannot suggest it enough!"

Jess Connolly, author of *You Are the Girl for the Job* and *Breaking Free from Body Shame*

"As a counselor to kids and families for almost three decades, I believe we've never walked through a season where moms feel more exhausted, more defeated, and more isolated than today. For years, I have been deeply grateful for Heather MacFadyen's voice. I've spoken with moms all over the country who have learned and laughed and grown with her through her podcast. I'm so grateful that voice is now in written form. And I'm so grateful for the truth that she shares in the words of her book, *Don't Mom Alone*. I believe this book will help you feel more known, more hopeful, freer to be honest, and certainly less alone in your courageous and transformative journey as a mom."

Sissy Goff, MEd, LPC-MHSP, director of child and adolescent counseling at Daystar Counseling Ministries, speaker, and author of *Raising Worry-Free Girls*

"Heather is the friend you need in your parenting corner who isn't afraid to join you in the trenches and offer encouragement and hope. Wise, warm, and relatable, Heather will guide you to truth every step of the way. *Don't Mom Alone* is the book for moms that you want to get for yourself and your best friend!"

Alli Worthington, business coach and bestselling
author of *Standing Strong*

"With deep insight, sympathy, and a healthy dose of humor, Heather puts her finger on the heartbeat of motherhood with grace and wisdom. She leads her readers to breathe in peace as they learn to leave the burden of motherhood in the hands of the One who companions them lovingly through their journey."

Sally Clarkson, bestselling author, host of the *At Home
with Sally* podcast, and mother and best friend
of four adult children

"Whether you have a newborn or a couple dozen grown children, every mother needs to read this book. From the priceless freedom found in chapter 1, Heather gently lifts the unnecessary burdens we carry, wraps her arms around our shoulders, and reminds us that we are never alone in this journey of motherhood. With vulnerability and laugh-out-loud humor, Heather shares practical wisdom and insight to help us trade lies for truth and isolation for connection. If you've ever wondered how to find the village that's supposed to help raise your child, this book is the map that will make sure you don't mom alone."

Kat Lee, author of *Hello Mornings* and
founder of HelloMornings.org

"For as long as I've known Heather, she has been inviting parents into community. An honest, life-giving community that is likely to involve laughter and tears, conversation and challenge, help and hope. This book is an extension of the rich community she has long created. The deeper you get into the pages of this work, the less alone you will feel and the more grace you will begin to extend to yourself. I want both of those things for every parent I spend time with in my counseling practice."

David Thomas, therapist and coauthor of bestsellers
Wild Things and *Are My Kids on Track?*

"Heather's creative energy, grace, challenges, insights, and human-ness leap off every page of this journey through real-life parenting. She weaves the bigness of God's grace and the richness of God's truth into everything from a thirty-foot-high bathroom accident at the museum to the grief of losing her father. Through it all, she draws on the wisdom of the Bible and her many mentors (she really doesn't mom alone!) to remind us of truth that connects us to each other, to God, and to our privileged calling as parents. Two thumbs up!"

Lynne and Jim Jackson, cofounders of Connected Families

Don't Mom Alone

GROWING THE RELATIONSHIPS YOU NEED TO
BE THE MOM YOU WANT TO BE

Heather MacFadyen

Revell

a division of Baker Publishing Group
Grand Rapids, Michigan

© 2021 by Heather C. MacFadyen

Published by Revell
a division of Baker Publishing Group
PO Box 6287, Grand Rapids, MI 49516-6287
www.revellbooks.com

Printed in the United States of America

Library of Congress Cataloging-in-Publication Data
Names: MacFadyen, Heather C., 1977– author.
Title: Don't mom alone : growing the relationships you need to be the mom you want to be / Heather MacFadyen.
Description: Grand Rapids, Michigan : Revell, a division of Baker Publishing Group, [2021]
Identifiers: LCCN 2021003922 | ISBN 9780800739324 (paperback) | ISBN 9780800741297 (casebound) | ISBN 9781493431977 (ebook)
Subjects: LCSH: Mother and child—Religious aspects—Christianity. | Motherhood—Religious aspects—Christianity. | Female friendship—Religious aspects—Christianity.
Classification: LCC BV4529.18 .M28 2021 | DDC 248.8/431—dc23
LC record available at https://lccn.loc.gov/2021003922

Some names and details have been changed to protect the privacy of the individuals involved.

Author is represented by The Christopher Ferebee Agency, www.christopherferebee.com.

Baker Publishing Group publications use paper produced from sustainable forestry practices and post-consumer waste whenever possible.

21 22 23 24 25 26 27   7 6 5 4 3 2 1

For my dad,
who left this earth before he could
read his favorite author's first book.
Thank you, Pops, for making it easy
to believe in a heavenly Father's love.
And for instilling purpose in my motherhood
with regular reminders
that the world needs more godly men.
Miss you tons,
Your Heather-bean

Contents

Foreword

There was a time when many of us would have lived in neighborhoods full of people who really knew each other. Homes were not just individual houses but instead were houses surrounded by a community of other homes. Families were in those homes. And holding those families together were mothers who primarily worked at home—cooking, cleaning, minding small children, and taking care of the business of the household.

They did this together.

At any given time, a mother could walk out her front door and knock on her neighbor's door for tea and conversation. She could work in her yard and talk to her neighbor over the fence or maybe walk across the street to get a cup of sugar. Moms physically and functionally experienced life together.

Many years have come and gone since the days when most mothers had the opportunity to know this kind of "together life." The majority of moms in America work outside the home, and most know very few, if any, of their neighbors. What does this mean for moms who used to know community in the places where they lived and spent much of their time?

It means they often feel as if they are doing motherhood alone.

Becoming a mom gives us the opportunity to know great love, but it also gives many of us the opportunity to feel isolated, overwhelmed, and lonely. With each year, our children grow from one season of development to the next, which means mothers are constantly stepping into new territory. Not only do we have to grow to parent our children, but we also have to learn to balance our responsibilities, our dreams, and the care we give to all the people we love. With the constant change and growth of our kids, many of us feel like we don't know what we're doing or whether we are doing it well.

Motherhood is a beautiful gift. However, the aspiration to be that rock for our children brings with it a heavy weight. Motherhood is work. It requires the giving of time and energy over the long haul. And when we have to carry the load of the motherhood journey by ourselves, the weight becomes greater.

I'm so grateful for my friend Heather MacFadyen and her awareness and sensitivity to this reality. For years, Heather has not only known about the need moms today have for community, encouragement, and practical help; she has done something about it. Through her podcast, Heather has shared her own wisdom and then gone one step further to bring in educators, therapists, psychologists, pastors, and seasoned parents to labor alongside her in her passion to serve moms well. Heather has served her audience by bringing messages that moms everywhere could listen to as they rocked children, mopped floors, commuted to and from work, went on their morning runs, or pushed strollers on their afternoon walks.

Now Heather brings years of her own parenting wisdom coupled with years of wisdom gained from hosting her podcast right here to the pages of this book.

Don't Mom Alone is your invitation to learn from mothers past who have mothered well and to stand with mothers present who seek to do the same. You are a mom who takes the role of motherhood seriously, and you want to be intentional in the journey of pouring into people. You are the mother *your* children need, and while there is only one of you—you are not standing alone.

And you don't have to mom alone either.

Welcome to your opportunity to be part of a "together kind of life." As you read these pages, you will know what it takes to engage in relationships that will help you be the mom you want to be. You will also begin to believe you really are part of a community of women who understand the beauty of motherhood and who are aiming to do it well.

Chrystal Evans Hurst, speaker, host of *Chrystal's Chronicles* podcast, and author of *She's Still There*

Preface

I don't like "mom" books.

It takes having a horrible day and hitting rock bottom to pick up a book on mothering.

Then when I do? After a few pages I set the book down on my bedside table. Throw my head back on the pillow as my mind fills with all the ways I fell short of the "good mom" mark that day.

Instead of feeling understood, I feel scolded. Layers of "should" piled on my shoulders.

I want you to know that I've had lots of bad parenting moments. I still have four children living under my roof. And I haven't a clue what it takes to turn out a decent human. Because for every formula I've been handed, I've found outlier kiddos whom the formula doesn't fit.

You'd also think I'd be more adept at building community if I was going to write a book about it. But I'm not inherently a team player. Going it alone is much more appealing. If I let other moms see my mess, then I can't keep up an image of perfection. If I admit that I need help, I show that I'm not enough to parent four boys. And what if my boys misbehave and others see the failure and reject me?

These isolating ideas have kept me from the relationships I need to be the mom I want to be. According to former US Surgeon General Dr. Vivek Murthy, isolation (a physical state) differs from loneliness (a subjective feeling). Of course, the number and type of relationships required to feel less lonely vary from person to person. He also noted that "isolation is considered a risk factor for loneliness simply because you are more likely to feel lonely if you rarely interact with others."[1] I don't think I'm the only one who'd prefer to isolate rather than lean on the village. Our modern American culture tends toward individualism rather than community living. Because of that, so many of us are carrying the heavy burden of mothering alone.

So instead of handing you a formula on how to be a competent mom (psst, it doesn't exist), I'm going to walk with you to address these isolating ideas and help you trade them for connecting truths. We'll start by dealing with internal lies, helping you to trust God more in your day-to-day challenges. Honestly, that may involve intentional solitude, which is very different from isolation. But it can be important for the healing necessary to engage others.

Once we've done the inner work, we'll move on to the people around you—friends, mentors, spouses—focusing on how to connect with them in healthy ways to get the support you need. Lastly, we'll tackle the four most common parenting challenges moms reach out to me for help with. I'll share wisdom from mentors in the areas of calm parenting, connected discipline, challenging children, and effective discipleship, because being the mom you want to be includes having meaningful relationships with your kids.

At the end of each chapter, you'll find questions to work through on your own, or even better, work through with a group of moms. Along the way I'll share my "Titanic" (avoid the iceberg ahead) stories and favorite resources. At the very end of the book you'll find a QR code you can scan to follow a link to my site. There you can listen to referenced or related podcast episodes for each chapter.

Perhaps, like me, you let the fears of rejection, pain, and failure keep you from taking a risk and being vulnerable. Or maybe you simply don't know how to add those relationships into an already full life. At the start of each chapter, you'll find short testimonials from moms who understand the struggle to choose connection over isolation.

The hope is not just to sit in the ditch with you but to give you a hand up, a way out. My friends say I'm a "reframer." I take their situation and bring perspective, faith, and hope. I want to do the same for you. Let's move from transparency to transformation. Because as my kids are becoming adults, I'm becoming a mom. Learning right alongside them. I need just as much patience and grace for my own maturation process as they do. Maybe you need that reminder too.

You wouldn't expect a newborn to walk out of the womb. Free yourself from the expectations that you will know exactly what to do in every scenario. Take each stage as it comes. When you don't know what to do, ask someone for help or perspective. Consider what you value and how it impacts your next step. Lastly, trust that God's power to redeem your mistakes is bigger than your power to destroy your children.

Are you ready to move forward? Take my hand; let's do this together and not mom alone.

Empowered by God

one

Let Him Be a Jerk

I have felt most isolated when there has been a concerning problem with one of my kids. I felt shame. Maybe people would think it was something we as parents did or didn't do.

—Tia

Guilty tears slid down my cheek.

My crime? Not letting my son be a jerk.

Let me explain.

I'd worked up the courage to take my two-year-old and newborn to the local arboretum. If you're picturing a peaceful garden experience, let me adjust that for you. The Dallas Arboretum in the fall is a madhouse. From crowded parking to walking a billion feet to arrive at the pecan orchard. I'm sweating a little just remembering the insanity.

Why would I subject myself to this rigmarole? To capture the perfect "kids in the pumpkin patch" picture, of course.

In only two years of motherhood, I had decided this would be our tradition. Come hell or high water, my kids would wear orange and sit on scratchy hay in front of a pile of pumpkins. They would look right at the camera. And be happy about it. Cuz that's what "good moms" do!

Last year, I'd invited mom friends to join me in attempting this feat. But adding another baby to the mix this year created a bit of complexity to coordinating schedules. I'd convinced myself it would be better if I just went by myself. Of course, I'd prepared for my mission, including remembering pre-pumped breast milk in a bottle.

As fate would have it, a large group of my church friends and their kiddos were also at the arboretum for a MOPS outing. I hadn't yet entered the Mothers of Preschoolers community, but I was intrigued.

Groups of moms wandered through hay bales looking for the perfect spot to plop their precious blessings. I saw mentors holding babies or offering to include the new mom in the pumpkin picture. One mom chased her three-year-old while her friend stood guard over the now-abandoned stroller.

With perfect fall weather, my boys dressed adorably, and nap time quickly approaching, I needed to stay focused on my goal. Just as I started to unstrap the baby, he wailed with the "I need to eat or I'm gonna die" scream. In classic multiple-kid style, my toddler added to the cacophony with his own grumpy complaints.

Preoccupied with the two-kid shuffle, I hadn't noticed that a mentor from my church approached my chaos. In a perfect British accent, she offered her help. And, of course, I told her I was "fine." (Narrator: Heather was far from fine.) Fortunately, she persisted and asked, "Does the toddler have a snack?"

A snack! Yes, that's it. The boy just needed a snack.

Balancing the bottle under my chin and cradling the newborn, I dug into the giant diaper bag desperate to show this mentor that as a "good mom" I had indeed packed a snack. She sweetly offered the snack to my oldest. To which he rudely responded with a harrumph, turning his head and body away from her.

I was horrified. How could my precious son respond with such disdain? And to a British woman, no less!

That's when I resorted to my go-to coping mechanisms of correction and excuses. "Quade, be kind!" Then, turning to the British woman, "I'm so sorry. He's ready for his nap and is overwhelmed by the crowd, and I think he may be teething." (Okay, maybe I didn't use teething this time, but it always was a good fallback excuse.)

The next part of the story is forever etched in my memory.

She looked me dead in the eyes and said (again with the accent), "Why as mothers do we feel like we need to apologize for our children? If he wants to be a jerk, let him be a jerk" (mic drop).

All I could do was cry.

Not happy, grateful tears for her transformational insight (which would stick with me fifteen years later). Nope. In my new mom state, I couldn't absorb her sage advice because I felt critiqued. Motherhood had become the focus of all my time, energy, and identity. So when an older mom pointed out a flaw in my approach, I took it as a direct assault.

In reality her correction wasn't directed toward my actions but highlighted the error in my thinking. I wrongly believed my son's emotional state and physical actions were my responsibility to control. When I offered an apology ("I'm sorry; he needs a nap.") it was because I felt responsible for his wrong attitude and behavior. If he was bad, I was bad. The umbilical cord remained metaphorically attached.

Now I *was* guilty of not letting my son be a jerk. But I wasn't guilty for his grumpy response. I had unnecessarily burdened myself with the idea that he would have behaved better if I had trained him differently. Or he would have been kinder if I had set him up for success with more sleep/snacks/etc. My actions directly contributed to his poor response.

23

In 1986, Melody Beattie wrote the trailblazing book *Codependent No More*. While written to help those in toxic relationships with addicts, her insights hit a little close to home when it came to my mothering. This quote basically sums up why I cried with the British woman:

> We don't have to take other people's behaviors as reflections of our self-worth. We don't have to be embarrassed if someone we love chooses to behave inappropriately. It's normal to react that way, but we don't have to continue to feel embarrassed and less than if someone else continues to behave inappropriately. Each person is responsible for his or her behavior.[1]

Of course I may get embarrassed by someone else's actions every now and then. The problem arises when I habitually believe others can't be held responsible for themselves. So often we are taught to be responsible for other people but not to be responsible for ourselves. This is compounded in motherhood. My energy shifted from controlling myself to being consumed with my child. It makes sense this happens. Codependency naturally sets in when a parent is required to care for an infant. Between middle-of-the-night feedings, constant diaper changes, and immobility, a newborn is totally dependent on someone else. As parents we often squelch our own desires in order to meet a child's needs.

Please understand that taking care of a child's needs is not rescuing or a problem. But in early motherhood I felt like my child's happy, content emotional state was an indicator of not only my performance as a mom but also my value and worth as a human. Like Beattie writes, "We don't feel lovable, so we settle for being needed."[2]

Bearing the weight of responsibility for my child's happiness and how he turns out is too much. Often I choose to carry that burden from a desire to be needed because I don't believe outside of that role I am lovable. The term "mom guilt" gets thrown around a lot. What I felt was closer to "mom shame." In my understanding, "guilt" is the feeling after doing something wrong. "Shame" is feeling "I am wrong." It's the difference between doing and being.

A grumpy child communicated to me that I was wrong. In response I bent over backward to keep my kids happy. The problem is the more kids you have, the harder this becomes. Until you finally take the advice of the British woman to "let him be a jerk" or eventually hit your limit. In my case, I chose the second option, which you can read more about in chapter 5.

But Can't My Kid Really Fail?

Perhaps you're fully aware that you can't make your child happy. But you're struggling a bit with the idea to "let him be a jerk." Am I (and a British woman) really suggesting we let kids run amok and be horrible human beings? No correction? No discipline? No care for what kind of adult he or she becomes? Absolutely not what I'm implying. Children need love, care, correction, and healthy boundaries. The key is that I can offer those things and release the responsibility of how my child behaves and who she or he becomes. Unfortunately, for many reasons this choice isn't easy.

I once heard a mentor speak to a group of type A moms, and she told us how she only started talking to moms about parenting after her children were grown and she knew she had not failed. While I respect her waiting to impart wisdom until her children were grown, I have a problem with her last phrase. By saying she "had not failed," she communicated to a room full of try-hard moms that they *could* fail.

While you and I try to shirk the responsibility for our child's emotional state and behavior, comments like this keep drawing that connection. Like the stereotypical psychologist's question: "Tell me about your mother." Or how we respond to a tragic public shooting. What's one of your first thoughts? Be honest. I usually want to know the shooter's story. Who are their parents?

What went wrong to produce a human who could do something so horrific?

I believe God has given us a responsibility to love our children well. To model grace, teach truth, and train love. But because of Adam and Eve in the garden, they are born sinners. Like Jennie Allen once said, "Don't pray your kids out of trouble. They'll get in trouble. Pray they get caught. Then let them feel all the trouble. You aren't trying to raise kids that don't sin. You are trying to raise kids that know they need God. So getting caught is the goal. Don't be shocked. Don't protect them from consequences."[3]

I agree 100 percent. I can't keep my children from failure. And I don't believe if they "fail" (whatever that means), they are beyond God's ability to redeem and use them. What if my boys need a "train wreck with grace" (my pastor's words) to truly grasp God's love?

My friend Tricia Goyer, who is an author of more than seventy books, encourages writers on how to balance life as a writer and mom. She has three grown biological children and six adopted children. Her past includes an abortion when she was fifteen years old. Her first son was born when she was seventeen, and the father left her.

Did her parents fail because of her teenage pregnancy? Was her life beyond God's restoration and His ability to use her to minister to others? I don't believe so. Her story only strengthened her faith, her ministry, and her passion for others to know Christ.

Another friend, Stacy, a vibrant woman of faith, has a history of drug use and rehab. On her flight to a Christian blogging conference she sat next to a seventeen-year-old boy. She was hoping to meet some women heading to the conference, but God had different plans.

Prompted by the Spirit and given her "failed" past, she asked the boy, "Do you like rap?" He responded, "Yah." Stacy boldly said, "Well, I'm a rapper." Right there on a plane she shared her broken story in a rap. Then he shared his. He had just come out of rehab and was going to live with his aunt. Because of her history and experience she was able to warn him to be on guard for more temptation.

You see, after she came out of rehab her family moved to a new city to get a fresh start. The first time she went out of the house alone, a man named Leon walked up to her and asked, "Do you know where I can get high?" In that moment of temptation, she spiraled down again. So she warned this seventeen-year-old recovering drug addict to "watch out for Leons." Advice that could save his life. Advice she was able to give only because she had been a "failure." I also imagine how God uses others to fill in the space we, as parents, can't fill. Stacy became a voice of reason for this boy, perhaps an answer to his parents' prayers.

Didn't God's perfect Son look like a "failure" as He hung on the cross? But we would not have access to God or be promised eternal life if Jesus had not carried the weight and shame of humanity's brokenness and failures. Any sin or failing in our own or our children's lives—past, present, future—was nailed to the cross. Yes, consequences are real. We experience pain and grief with the loss of dreams we hold for our kids. But our hope isn't found in a successful child; it is found in a faithful God. When I believe the lie that I am fully responsible for my child's outcome, I miss out on deeper dependence on Jesus.

Important, but Not Essential

Thankfully the connection between parenting and how our kids turn out doesn't have to be negative. In the book of Exodus, Moses's mom, Jochebed, devised a genius plan to save his life. "Then Pharaoh gave this order to all his people: 'Every Hebrew boy that is born you must throw into the Nile, but let every girl live'" (Exod. 1:22). She hid Moses for three months. Then when he couldn't be hidden any longer (aka, babbling baby), she placed him in a fancy tar-lined basket, paid attention to when Pharaoh's daughter bathed, and set up her daughter in the reeds to offer care for the baby.

> Then his sister asked Pharaoh's daughter, "Shall I go and get one of the Hebrew women to nurse the baby for you?"
>
> "Yes, go," she answered. So the girl went and got the baby's mother. Pharaoh's daughter said to her, "Take this baby and nurse him for me, and I will pay you." So the woman took the baby and nursed him. When the child grew older, she took him to Pharaoh's daughter and he became her son. (Exod. 2:7–10)

What did I tell you—genius! Not only did she keep her baby alive, she got paid to do it!

So, was Jochebed important in the outcome of Moses's life? Absolutely!

Based on the culture of the time, children were nursed until around five years of age. What I find valuable is how influential those five years were for Moses. He spent the rest of his childhood in a palace where idol worship reigned. Yet, after fleeing for his life, he recognized Yahweh in the burning bush. He dedicated his life to serving the One True God and helping free God's chosen people.

This dedication to a Hebrew God came from only five years with his Jewish mother. Those little years mattered! Mothering babies, toddlers, preschoolers matters.

Consider another biblical icon: Samuel. In 1 Samuel 1:11, his mother, Hannah, pleaded for a child. She promised, if given one, she would give that child back to God. God answered her prayer with the birth of Samuel. She kept her promise by allowing him to live in the temple with the priest Eli. But only after she had finished nursing him (again, about five years of a faithful mom loving her son). And we read that Samuel lived a life dedicated to the service of the Lord. He heard God's voice and prophesied to the people. He listened to God in choosing King David—a vital detail in God's bigger story.

Never underestimate the value of cuddling with your babies. Meeting their physical, emotional, and social needs. Realizing that the concept of love begins in your home. And no other person you minister to on this planet will know you more intimately than your children. You are so important.

But I can't stop there because I know my friend Kat Lee's story. She has an incredible ministry helping women create a habit of waking up a little bit earlier to plan their day, move their bodies, and spend time with God. I'm one of those women.

Her work pulled me out of a dark season of motherhood. Back then, every morning I rolled out of bed right as my husband left for work. I grumbled in the kitchen as three little boys pleaded for a second breakfast. The remainder of the day felt like a constant bombardment of responding to needs. I found myself completely burnt out and miserable in the exact role I'd always wanted.

That's when Kat (and God) entered the story. Through her Hello Mornings ministry and personal encouragement, I started waking up just five minutes earlier than my kids.[4] Read a verse, said a prayer, did a push-up (don't judge), and looked at my calendar. The small habit grew into a well of refreshment. God began to download His thoughts on my mothering experience. I started to write out those truths on a blog that I called *God Centered Mom*. It was the start of a ministry He had in store for me. A ministry that wouldn't have happened if it weren't for Kat.

Here's why I bring up my friend. Her mom passed away when Kat was a baby. Her desire to help women came from her own season of worn-out motherhood. A fact that surprised her, since she desperately wanted to be the mom she never had. She knew the importance of a mother's role. That void mattered. But her mom wasn't essential to Kat being used by God for His purposes. God had good plans set aside in advance for Kat to do. He wasn't surprised that she would live a life without her biological mother.

That is the tension we hold in order to walk in freedom as moms. My friend Jennie Cunnion said it this way in her *Mom Set Free*

Bible study: "I am significant in my kids' lives but I am not sovereign, God is."[5]

My Part, God's Part

During those morning moments in God's Word inspired by Kat, I started a simple practice. While reading a verse I paid attention to any commands or invitations and any mention of God's promises or character. I noted that the command or invitation is my responsibility. The promise or revelation of God's character lets me know His response. I'd underline my part in one color and God's part in another color. What surprised me was how often "my part" was more about my heart and faith. And how God took care of the bigger responsibilities—like future outcomes.

Here are some examples:

> "Let the one who boasts boast about this:
>   that they have the understanding to know me,
>   that I am the LORD, who exercises kindness,
>   justice and righteousness on earth,
>   for in these I delight," declares the Lord. (Jer. 9:24)

My part: to understand and know God, that He is "I AM" (Yahweh).

His part: to exercise kindness, justice, and righteousness.

> For God so loved the world that he gave his one and only Son, that whoever believes in him shall not perish but have eternal life. (John 3:16)

My part: to believe in God's Son, Jesus.

His part: to love the world, to give His only Son, to provide eternal life.

> I waited patiently for the LORD;
>   he turned to me and heard my cry.

30

He lifted me out of the slimy pit,
  out of the mud and mire;
he set my feet on a rock
  and gave me a firm place to stand. (Ps. 40:1–2)

My part: to wait patiently and cry out.

His part: to turn to me, hear me, lift me out of a pit/mud/mire, set my feet on a rock, and give me a firm place to stand.

Doesn't it feel better to do your part and let God do His? In doing so, you and I can release the "mom shame" of being unlovable or unworthy if a kid behaves badly. And it doesn't stop there. Turns out we can drop some of the "mom guilt" too.

Dr. John Townsend tells the story of how at a speaking event a mom asked the question, "How much of what my child becomes is my fault?" He and his coauthor, Dr. Henry Cloud (both licensed psychologists), looked at each other and decided to play a little game. They went to separate sides of the stage and each wrote on a piece of paper what percentage a child was responsible and what percentage a parent contributed to a child's outcome. When they turned the pieces of paper around, they had written the same numbers.

What do you think they wrote? Zero percent kid, 100 percent mom? Fifty/fifty? Did they agree with what I've presented here?

(Drumroll, please.)

Based on their clinical anecdotal evidence, they both felt a child was 70 percent responsible and a mom contributed 30 percent. Thirty percent! My mentor Diane used to tell me, "If I take credit for the good, I have to take credit for the bad." Turns out we can take credit for 30 percent of the bad and the good. But, of course, there's a catch.

Marketer John Wanamaker famously said, "Half the money I spend on advertising is wasted; the trouble is I don't know which half."[6] Therein lies the rub. I may be only 30 percent responsible, but I don't know which 30 percent. Thankfully I do know that God is willing to fill in the gaps if I let Him.

Instead of believing the isolating idea that I'm fully responsible for how my kids turn out and my value and identity are wrapped up in their outcome, I'm choosing to connect with God by remembering I'm important but not essential. Focusing on my part—to love, guide, connect with my kids—and letting Him do His part—to fulfill the purposes He has ordained in advance. Believing that God is fully capable to redeem and restore my kids. If He chooses not to do so this side of heaven, I can trust that He loves them more than I can imagine. By not blaming Him or myself, but instead turning to God, I can find comfort grieving *with* Him. Then I can move forward in the purposes He planned in advance for me to do. And let my kid be a jerk.

Isolating Idea
I am fully responsible for my child's outcome.

Connecting Truth
I am important but not essential in God's plan for my child.

Discussion Questions

1. Share about a time when you have tied your child's performance to your ability as a mom.
2. In what ways do you bear the burden of your child's happiness? How does that impact other relationships?

3. Have you ever considered how as mothers we are important but not essential to the plans God has set in advance for our kids?

4. Waking up a few minutes before my kids was transformational for me. What is a small habit you can start today to remember God's truth of who you are and who He is?

5. Read Ephesians 2:8–10 and consider what part of this verse is yours and what part is God's.

two

Mother of the Year

For me, isolation in motherhood looks like feeling like I am
doing a job in which I am so incompetent. The feeling that I
am doing something wrong in my mothering goes alongside
the isolation. Which sends me into a spiral of deeper isolation because talking about my failure feels scary. Yet, that
is generally the fix for getting out of the negative spiral.

—Daniella

"Can you find a picture of something that starts with 'tuh'?"

I couldn't help but notice how the parents in front of me created
ways to entertain their five-year-old on a flight to Dallas. Using the
in-flight magazine to not only occupy his attention but teach him
phonics. When the boy began to whine, they calmly redirected him.

Any parent can understand the stress of flying with young children. Confined space. Other people's expectations for quiet, controlled behavior. And a child coping with a completely unfamiliar

35

situation. All of which leads to an epic meltdown (for the child and parent).

Whenever I am flying alone and witness families with children, my empathy radar goes way up. I smile a lot to reassure them. I may offer to help hold something or play peek-a-boo with a baby to be a helpful distraction. I always want to verbalize encouragement. In the case of this couple educating their five-year-old, I kept looking for a (non-awkward) opportunity to congratulate them on a job well done.

When we landed in Dallas, they stood up to deplane and the mom realized her son had peed in his pants. Horrified, she looked me straight in the eye and sarcastically said, "Mother of the Year."

If we'd known each other better, I would have taken hold of her hands and said, "*Yes!* Congratulations! You are the mother of the year. You just handled your son with grace, truth, and love for a long flight. You didn't become unglued when you realized you'd missed your connecting flight and would be spending a night in an airport hotel (okay, so I eavesdropped a bit too). I'd love to hand you an award because you are worthy of honor."

But instead, I just smiled and said, "Y'all are doing a great job!"

My Turn . . . with Worms

I'll never forget standing in the kitchen and hearing my son yell from the bathroom, "Hey, mom! You want to come see the worms in my poop? I named them!"

Excuse me, *what?*

Holding my nose, I peered down into the toilet to confirm his claim. Sure enough, a couple of little white strings started wiggling, and I almost vomited on top of them. This son (who shall go nameless for his protection) proceeded to tell me this was not the first time he'd seen worms in his poop. In his mind, he assumed it was normal. Again, *what?*

Immediately I googled "little white worms in poop" and discovered my son had pinworms. The suggested treatment involved medication, intense cleaning of the house, wiping his bottom each morning (since the female worms lay eggs at night . . . wish I was kidding), cutting his fingernails shorter, and washing his hands thoroughly after using the bathroom.

As I scrubbed his fingernails with a brush and antibacterial soap, he shared with me the names of his worm friends: Dale, William, Bobby, Wayne (Wayne is his favorite) . . . seriously.

My inner critic taunted me with "MOTHER OF THE YEAR!!!"

In that moment it seemed harvesting worms in our bodies was hitting rock bottom. The mothering doubts rolled in. Had I not bathed him enough? Forced him to wash his hands after using the bathroom? Prohibited putting rocks in his mouth?

Then I remembered the mom from the airplane and how she had thrown the proverbial "baby out with the bath water." I wondered, *How do we keep that baby and lose the bad water?* From the last chapter, perhaps I've convinced you to release full responsibility for how your child turns out. But what about the daily dos and don'ts of motherhood with each of us feeling like we constantly fall short of an unattainable standard?

Good Mom Formula

Maybe you can relate. In just a few minutes at home with little ones, my eyes are scanning the room with my mind repeating the lie:

Boys squabbling over a LEGO Minifigure. Failure as a mom.
Piles of laundry demanding attention. Failure as a homemaker.
Hand weights acting more like doorstops than exercise equipment. Failure as a woman.

23,456 emails waiting to be read. Failure as an entrepreneur and friend.

In my fifteen years of being a mom, I've read countless books, sought the counsel of mentors, swapped ideas with mom friends, pinned creative snack ideas, listened to podcasts, attended mom conferences, and interviewed seven years' worth of weekly guests on my podcast, *Don't Mom Alone*. I still wouldn't give myself the "good mom" title. Not to mention, I haven't found a step-by-step guide for success.

Many days have ended with a tear-filled, self-deprecating monologue (usually in the kitchen). It never went well when my husband encouraged me to "care a little less" or "stop trying so hard."

One night I vividly remember him saying, "Is there any mom who thinks she's doing a good job?"

Stop traffic. Is there?

Now, I've never met a mom who wants to fail or who intentionally plans to do a bad job. Most gals I interact with want to do a good job. To be a good friend. To be a good wife. To have a good life. But no mom comes to mind who honestly believes she's attained these goals. She often feels they fall just out of reach. Or as she's mastered one, the other ten drop. Moms often come to my website or podcast looking for the perfect mothering method. Hoping somehow I can hand them a "good mom" formula and send them on their way.

I get it. When my son at eighteen months old still didn't sleep through the night, I was desperate. Scouring books and resources, I looked for any way to solve my parenting problem. Wouldn't you know I found three books with vastly different sleep-training methods. And each claimed to be the "good" option and disparaged the others.

It was an epiphany moment. If experts couldn't agree on how to help a toddler sleep through the night, then how could I believe there was one recipe for raising a child?

Here's the truth: there is no "good mom" formula.

Redefining Good

If you've watched the movie *The Princess Bride*, you remember the famous line from Inigo Montoya as he corrected his boss, Vizzini: "You keep using that word. I don't think it means what you think it means."[1] My tendency is to act as if "good" means acceptable to others, correct, and right. Unfortunately, with that definition, the standard keeps moving. From one culture to the next, one generation to the next, the consensus of "good" differs.

In April 2019, I traveled with a group of women to meet migrants traveling through Mexico. Our first night I sat on my hotel bed crying in anticipation of meeting unaccompanied children in the migrant center. When your entire ministry is focused on moms, there is deep grief at the thought of a child living life without a mother. I had braced myself for that kind of sadness. What I hadn't anticipated was meeting an eleven-year-old with her one-week-old baby. My sunglasses couldn't conceal the tears slipping down my cheeks. An eleven-year-old doesn't choose to become a mom. A child birthing a child doesn't seem "good" to me. Yet she stood there with pride holding her precious tiny one. And I gave her a hug and honestly told her in my high-school-level Spanish that she's a "good mom."

I also met a fourteen-year-old from Honduras living in the migrant center with her eight-month-old baby. We chatted with the help of a translator, her son comfortably settled on her hip. His arms draped around her neck. The longer we talked, the lower his eyelids dropped until he fell asleep in her arms. For reals. In all my mothering days I don't think I've ever had a baby boy fall asleep in my arms when I'm standing up. Let alone while I had a conversation with a person from another country. Once again, in circumstances we would not deem "good," I hugged that precious mom and told her what God longed to tell her: "You're a good mom."

It was a clarifying moment for me. How often I complicate motherhood! Adding "should," programs, and guilt. Motherhood in that migrant center was simplified to this: love, connection, and care. Any mom advice you are given that doesn't also ring true for those sweet girls in Mexico? It's not necessary.

Not Perfection, but Holy Intention

Let's go back to my husband Bruce's question, "Does any mom think she is doing a good job?" Before I could answer, he asked another one: "Why do you think moms are so hard on themselves?"

I offered, "Perhaps it's the enormity of the job. It's not like laying bricks or making coffee. There is no assurance we are moving in the right direction. Having never done the job before, it's hard to know what's 'right,' and so we look around at how our friends do the same job. Then we read manuals on how others think we should do this job (sometimes contradictory approaches). We fall on our face, cry, and mess up a lot."

That's when Bruce kindly responded, "Can I just say I think you are doing a fabulous job? The fact that you care so much and want to read books and learn about how to be a great mom. Doesn't that inherently mean you are doing a better job than most moms?"

(He's a good man and he makes a good point.)

We do care.

That's why after losing my patience with my boys, I feel a mix of guilt and shame. The regrets worsen when my head hits the pillow. I recount the mistakes of the day, the ways I could have listened better, played more, and yelled less. **Because I care about their hearts.**

I scroll through Instagram and see the best version of "that" mom and fall way short. Focusing on the one area of motherhood she has mastered yet ignoring the three or four other areas in which she struggles. I try to be all the kinds of moms at once: crafty mom, organized mom, fun mom, healthy mom, spiritual mom, and patient mom. **Because I care about their experiences.**

I pick up my middle child from preschool and hear he visited the director's office twice in one five-hour day, questioning all our discipline methods. Maybe he needs more consequences, or maybe if I connected to his heart more, or _____ (fill in the blank). **Because I care about who they are becoming.**

I hear my boys complain because the free toy that came in their Happy Meal wasn't the one they wanted. They whine for one more piece of candy. They beg to watch another movie. I feel the weight of raising entitled children. **Because I care about their characters.**

I read how I should pray more and say less. And think about how "that" family has a morning devotion time. I've pinned a link to memory verses for every letter of the alphabet. Maybe the problem with our family is we aren't religious enough. **Because I care about their souls.**

Author Graham Cooke said, "God has called you to see the invisible and do the impossible. God has not called you to do the things you can do. He's called you to do the things that you'll never be able to do in a billion years. This great God that we serve will throw us into situations beyond us with no other thought than His great heart will sustain us."[2]

What a privilege to be challenged so beyond my ability that I must rely on our great God. Because if I could be a great mom on my own, then I wouldn't need God. I would miss out on working with Him to grow these children into adults—to cheerlead them into the kingdom.

I found great comfort in these words from A. W. Tozer's book *The Pursuit of God*:

> "Them that honour me I will honour," said God once to a priest of Israel, and that ancient law of the Kingdom stands today unchanged by the passing of time or the changes of dispensation. . . .
>
> Sometimes the best way to see a thing is to look at its opposite. Eli and his sons are placed in the priesthood with the stipulation that they honor God in their lives and ministrations. This they *fail* to do, and God sends Samuel to announce the consequences. Unknown to Eli this law of reciprocal honor has

been all the while secretly working, and now the time has come for judgment to fall. Hophni and Phineas, the degenerate priests, fall in battle, the wife of Hophni dies in childbirth, Israel flees before her enemies, the ark of God is captured by the Philistines and the old man Eli falls backward and dies of a broken neck. Thus stark tragedy followed upon Eli's failure to honor God.

Now set over against this almost any Bible character who honestly *tried* to glorify God in his earthly walk. See how God *winked at weaknesses and overlooked failures* as He poured upon His servants grace and blessing untold. Let it be Abraham, Jacob, David, Daniel, Elijah or whom you will; honor followed honor as harvest the seed. The man of God set his heart to exalt God above all; God accepted his intention as fact and acted accordingly. *Not perfection, but holy intention made the difference.*[3]

Tozer is pointing out Eli's legitimate failure and real consequences. He's also noting that for a majority of biblical characters, God overlooked failures and instead poured out blessing. Don't misunderstand what I'm saying as preaching prosperity gospel. I'm also not trying to claim that those who experience tragedy must not have honored God.

The words that encouraged me were "any Bible character who honestly tried to glorify God . . ."

Oh sister. I'm trying.

"God winked at weaknesses and overlooked failures as He poured upon His servants grace and blessing untold."

I don't know about you, but I could use a few winks at my weaknesses and a hefty pouring of grace. I know my family appreciates when the tone around our home is one of grace and not shame.

You know what's easy for me to see? The mistakes. But it's harder for me to remember that where sin is, grace is even bigger (Rom. 5:20). When our family was recovering from a season of loss and recalibrating from a critical tone, our parenting coach, Lynne

Jackson from Connected Families, recommended when someone made a mistake we happily declare, "Grace is bigger!"

Yes, there are consequences to sin. And yes, as best as we can we right the wrong. But God isn't looking down with a magnifying glass to catch us when we mess up. Instead, He's inviting us to remember how we can embrace the good news of His daily, abundant grace. Mistakes give us an opportunity to learn, to forgive, and to repair.

"Not perfection, but holy intention made the difference."

Your intention to honor God in mothering matters. Your desire to please Him and treat Him special in your home is noticed by our Holy God. He sees you trying. He sees me trying. And He winks at our weaknesses. He overlooks failures. And He pours grace over us.

And as I accept that truth, I'm able to present my imperfect, well-intentioned self to you. I can show up to my community as I am. Not polished and filtered, fearful of judgment, but surrendered to God's redeeming work and His surrounding, amazing grace.

Isolating Idea
I am falling short of the good mom formula.

Connecting Truth
*I embrace my intention and release fear
of imperfection.*

Discussion Questions

1. What is something that went wrong today and you claimed to be a "failure"? Now, make a list of all the wonderful things that have gone well today (including meeting basic needs).

2. Do you feel like you do a good job? What area of motherhood are you wanting to do perfectly? Whose standard are you trying to keep?

3. Make a list of what you consider to be part of a "good mom" formula. Would these things work for the teen mom in Mexico?

4. Look at your "good mom" list and next to each item write out your heart's intention. What does it show you care about? How does it feel to acknowledge your intention instead of your imperfection?

three

Hole in My Bucket

As a stay-at-home mom I have school drop-offs/pickups, preschool drop-off/pickup, baby schedule, grocery shopping, errands, doctor appointments, etc. I'm busy and out seeing people but it's all transactional. My focus is on getting kids and getting what I need. So I can go day after day being surrounded by people, but never any more connection beyond, "How are you today? Do you need a bag for ten cents?" and if I'm lucky, "Have a nice day."

—CK

Living in Dallas, you don't dare go outside during the summer unless you are about to jump in a pool. Fortunately, there are several indoor entertainment options. One day I chose to take my boys to the flight museum. A way to entertain my three-year-old and one-year-old while my twenty-eight-weeks-pregnant body enjoyed the A/C. I packed a lunch so we could stay until nap time.

Everything went according to my well-thought-out plan. We admired the huge WWII planes, checked out a space shuttle pod, learned about fighter jets, and walked inside a real Southwest 747. Honestly, I felt like I was winning the mommy game—educating my little guys while hugely pregnant.

To reward myself, I sat down in a row of three airplane seats watching my sons explore a play area. Resting didn't last long as my toddler attempted to climb a set of stairs into a pretend airplane and lost his balance, nearly falling backward. I caught him just as I heard my three-year-old yell out, "Mommy, I go pee-pee!"

As every mom of a "potty-trained" child knows, his warning cry meant, "Drop everything and immediately proceed to the nearest bathroom." Unfortunately, as I searched for the source of his voice, I looked up to find him at the top of a thirty-foot-tall pretend flight tower.

Uninhibited by parents surrounding me, I yelled back, "You need to go pee-pee? Or you are going pee-pee?" I got my answer as I saw a stream of liquid flowing down all the levels of the playscape. I ran in my fastest waddle pace toward the base of the flight tower and pushed aside a little boy before he entered the deluge of fluid.

I glanced back to make sure my toddler was safe and not dangling from some high ledge. Then I decided to embark on the embarrassing rescue mission. Squeezing my pregnant body up through this series of overlapping, triangular platforms (think McDonald's playscape) that were now covered in pee, I retrieved my crying, soaking-wet three-year-old.

With some gentle, loving words, mixed in with some screechy whys, I carried him back down the flight tower. You read that right, not only did I maneuver my body through tight spaces, but I did so while carrying a wiggly, wet, and now screaming child.

He screamed because my little guy didn't like his clothes to be wet. When I say "didn't like," I mean, he hated it. He was unwilling to move an inch because each time he moved he felt the wetness in a new spot on his legs.

I emerged and immediately scanned the play area to find my toddler. Thankfully a kind mother kept an eye on him while I performed my rescue (Don't mom alone!). After thanking her, I scooped up the toddler, while still carrying the screaming preschooler, and made a beeline for the bathroom.

Fortunately (to look for a silver lining), I spotted one of those family options. I kicked open the door and began the cleanup process. Squatting on the floor, I stripped off the wet clothes and used paper towels to clean his sticky legs.

Preoccupied with the task at hand, I didn't notice my toddler had wandered over to the toilet. The moment I happened to glance back and check on him was the exact moment his pacifier-on-a-string dangled right into the not-so-shiny porcelain bowl.

Jumping up, I grabbed him right before he started to play in the toilet water. In another quick move, I snatched the pacifier clip off his shirt and tossed it in the nearby sink. Water cranked to the hottest possible level, I attempted to clean off what I imagined to be every microscopic organism ever discovered.

Once that fire appeared to be out, I squatted back down to appease my crying three-year-old. Since he had been "potty trained" (Have you noticed the quotes? Y'all get it) for almost a year, I no longer carried an extra change of clothes or underwear. My only option at this point was to place his brother's size-four diaper on him.

Unfortunately, while I was bent over, with huge belly and legs cramping, the toddler's newfound amusement was his mom. He began to "undo" the braid in my hair. The act of messing up my hair was not a big deal in itself, but in that particular moment given my frazzled state, I lost it.

Out-of-place hair was another reminder of my out-of-control life. I couldn't even have my hair in a braid without someone coming along to pull out chunks. It was a metaphor of motherhood in my mind. Children peeing in public places, giant pregnant bellies squeezing through tight spaces, pacifiers dangling in toilets, and personal appearance disheveled. Each event multiplied the feeling that my life no longer belonged to me.

The humiliation, the chaos, and the constant needs brought me to my knees in this family-size restroom. Instead of embracing motherhood, I threw a mommy tantrum. I asked why he didn't tell me he had to go to the bathroom, and I was frustrated at the busy, active nature of my toddler. But my boys weren't acting out of evil hearts. They were just being a three-year-old and a one-year-old.

In that moment with my pregnant body squatting on the bathroom floor to help clean up my pee-stained preschooler, I felt weary. Legit weary. And as funny as it is to recount now, I think I cried on the car ride home. Overwhelmed with the thought of adding one more person to this mix.

My inner monologue taunted me with "If I'm this tired now, how in the world can I manage more?" (Narrator: At this point Heather had no idea a fourth boy was in her future.) Little did I know how many more embarrassing and helpless scenarios it would take to change that question from "How can I manage more?" to "What can I give to God to manage?"

The reality of raising lots of little kids is that there will be moments when more is asked of you than you are capable of doing. Because I am a limited human being, I can only respond to one emergency at any given time. I don't actually have eyes in the back of my head.

Standing in the River

The gift of being a woman of faith is that I have a real Rescuer. Not just a flannel-board Sunday school story about a distant God but a legitimate, intimate Savior. Because of His great love for me, He promises to never leave me alone. And "never" includes forever. Spending eternity with God gives me more hope than having content, safe, happy kids.

But God didn't decide to rescue us in a moment. He sent His Son as a vulnerable human baby. One who grew on this planet and felt what you and I feel, familiar with suffering and pain. He doesn't observe from a distance.

In those legitimate, difficult mom moments, I can be confident God doesn't love me from afar but enters my story. He intimately understands the challenges I face. Joanna Weaver, in her book *Having a Mary Heart in a Martha World*, noted that Jesus experienced pain (John 11:35), poverty (Matt. 8:20), temptation (Mark 1:13), frustration (John 2:15–16), disappointment (Luke 13:34), ridicule (Mark 15:19), even loneliness (Matt. 27:46).[1]

If you feel weary, Jesus has felt weary. John 4:6 says, "Jesus, tired as he was from the journey, sat down by the well." Here we find Jesus with a woman who felt alone in her story. And Jesus asked her for a drink. She was shocked because of their different (and clashing) cultural groups: Jews vs. Samaritans. Before she could act and get Him what He asked for, she had to deal with the belief that she was disqualified. The first barrier being the location of her birth—something completely out of her control.

Jesus kindly told her that if she had known who was asking her (the God of the universe, who places people in families), she could have asked Him and He would have given *her* living water. In fact, her past did not disqualify her, but it qualified her for even more than she could imagine. In exchange for her act of service, she would receive life-giving, never-ending provision. "Everyone who drinks of this water will be thirsty again, but whoever drinks of the water that I will give him will never be thirsty again" (John 4:13–14 ESV).

The same is true in my mothering. God isn't saying to meet with Him each morning so I can be filled up and then poured out (like my son's pee spilling down through the playscape . . . Sorry, I couldn't resist). Jesus invites me to meet Him at the well. To be reminded of His *limitless* resources, outside of myself and my effort. Living water.

My friend Katie Sherrod (mom to eleven kiddos, several adopted) shared with me that at one point she worried about running out of love for her biological children if she also cared for foster kids or adopted more. God showed her He doesn't provide a pitcher of love but a river. Then He gave her the picture of her standing in His river of love as she simply invited her family to join her in it.[2]

The habit I'd developed of reading God's Word and praying each morning was less about being filled up to pour out and more about being reminded of the source of my love. The kind of love that Sally Lloyd-Jones calls "Never-stopping, Never Giving Up, Unbreaking, Always and Forever Love."[3]

Remember Psalm 23. David doesn't write about how God gives him a nice tall glass of ice-cold water to restore his soul. He refers to being led beside "waters of rest" (see footnote on Ps. 23:2 in the ESV). David also writes, "As the deer pants for streams of water, so my soul pants for you" (Ps. 42:1). Streams flow continuously. There is a longing in all of us for more than just quick satisfaction, but lasting, life-giving nourishment.

If I rely on ten minutes or even an hour of "quiet time" to fill me up enough to give to my needy crew, I'm gonna be bone-dry empty by 9:00 a.m. But if I remind myself in the morning and then keep going back to what I've read, I'm better able to invite my people into God's limitless supply of love, joy, peace, patience, kindness, and gentleness.

As Needed

Before experiencing it, I would have thought a dinner party with strangers was a terrible idea. What if I don't like who's there? Or worse, what if they don't like me? Would we stare at our plates while slowly taking bites of chicken? What would we talk about?

That last question was answered when Bruce handed me a little booklet. "Apparently we're all going to read this essay by Adam Smith called 'Theory of Moral Sentiments' and discuss it over dinner." Okay, so we have a common topic. But who is Adam Smith again?

As the mom to two young children, pregnant with my third, I already felt a bit like my brain had been on hold for a few years. I don't know how this is who I became. Kind of snuck up on me really. I'd read that a pregnant woman's brain shrinks and doesn't return to its original size until the baby is six months old.

So here I am with my shrunken brain, insecure and unsure of what insights I could bring to a conversation on free market economy. By God's grace, the seating plan had me sitting next to a fascinating woman, Kay Wyma. She commented on my pregnant state and shared that she had four older children and a surprise fifth born just two years ago. Immediately I breathed out my fears. I had a companion in this dinner adventure who understood motherhood.

Not only could she sympathize with my pregnant state, she shared encouragement about having more than two kids. Beyond that, she engaged the conversation on Adam Smith with intelligence and insight, which inspired me to join in as well. Who better to provide thoughts on society being "connected by sympathy" and "empathetic regard for the interest of others" than two moms?[4]

I later found out that before moving to Dallas and starting a family, Kay worked as an international banker and held several positions at the White House. God knew I needed to meet a woman who didn't lose herself in motherhood. That it was one of the roles He'd given her but not all of who she was.

Fast-forward a couple years and our paths crossed again when my husband and I were looking for a school to send our oldest son to. Dallas has a plethora of school options. The one I was about to walk into intimidated me. I worried our family didn't fit the mold. We weren't wealthy enough, "Dallas" enough, connected enough. Wouldn't you know, once again when insecurity started to grip my heart, God provided what I needed. Standing behind the front

51

desk welcoming parents to the open house event was none other than Kay. In my mind she represented "normal" and easy to know. And if her family went to this school then maybe mine could too.

Six years later in early December 2017, my parents had moved in with us. My mom had been diagnosed with breast cancer and just started treatment. A few days later, we learned my dad had liver cancer. In the hustle and bustle of the holidays, bleary-eyed I made my way down the school hallways. And standing in front of me was Kay. She listened to my long list of burdens. Then she slipped a simple bracelet off her wrist and onto mine. A black cord centered with a silver "O" charm. She said, "When you start to feel stress taking you down, I want you to look at this bracelet and be overwhelmed with Christ instead of your circumstances." Those words carried me through the next month.

While I sat by my dad's side and we counted his last breaths, Kay thoughtfully dropped off a cooler full of food at my house. Milk, bread, frozen PB&Js. She didn't ask, "What can I do?" or "What do you need?" She delivered what she thought I would need without my asking her to do it.

Friends, that's like our God. Yes, He is an unending source of living water. A river where we can invite others to join us. But He's more. He's our daily Provider. The One who gives us what we need, as needed.

My brother's mentor, Grammie (yes, he's a single fortysomething man with an older female mentor), shared a phrase that got her through a hard season. When she was caring for the needs of her aging mother, she listened to the old song "One Day at a Time, Sweet Jesus." That simple chorus helped her work through her challenges, one day at a time.

There's another woman who had to learn this lesson of daily dependence. Although she isn't named, her story is told in the book of 1 Kings. She was living alone with her son in the middle of a drought. She was out gathering a few sticks to take home and make a meal for herself and her son, so they could "eat it—and die"

(1 Kings 17:12). Her path crossed with Elijah, who had just had his daily needs met by some birds as he sat by a stream . . . true story. God told him to go to this widow in Zarephath. The first time in the Bible that a minister of God was sent specifically to a Gentile.

Like Jesus at the well, Elijah asked the woman to bring him some water. But there's more. As she went to get the water, he asked for some bread. This is when she let him know how little she had left to give: a handful of flour and a little olive oil.

Elijah encouraged her and instructed her: "Don't be afraid. Go home and do as you have said. But first make a small loaf of bread for me from what you have and bring it to me, and then make something for yourself and your son. For this is what the LORD, the God of Israel, says: 'The jar of flour will not be used up and the jug of oil will not run dry until the day the LORD sends rain on the land'" (1 Kings 17:13–14).

Okay, what would you do? Feed you and your child one last meal *or*, in faith, give away the little you have in hopes that God will provide an unlimited supply of what you need?

Well, this woman believed. She went and did what Elijah said to do. And because of her faith and obedience, she witnessed a miracle. Their lives were spared.

Perhaps it was seeing that miracle that led her to search for Elijah when tragedy struck again. Her son became ill and stopped breathing. Instead of asking Elijah for help, in her grief she accused him. "What do you have against me, man of God? Did you come to remind me of my sin and kill my son?" (1 Kings 17:18).

Elijah carried the boy upstairs and then questioned God: "Have you brought tragedy on this woman I am staying with?" (1 Kings 17:20). And this is where it got a little odd; he lay on top of the boy three times. Then he cried out, "LORD my God, let this boy's life return to him!" (v. 21). And the boy began to breathe again. Incredible.

Sometimes I discount miracles as being impossible today and set them back only into biblical times. Other times I consider my request for "a little more patience" unworthy of bothering God. Or the real barrier, what if I ask for God's help and nothing happens?

You see, I believe God is capable of doing the miraculous. But often I let myself struggle and manage on my own, when I *could* invite God into those weary moments. Like the widow, if I don't lean in with faith, I miss out on the miracle. What God is most interested in is my dependence and leaving the "how" of provision up to Him.

With the story of Elijah and the boy, God's power was made known through a simple prayer. With a sentence, empowered by the God who first created life, a child was resurrected.

A breath prayer that brought the breath of life.

What is a "breath prayer"? I consider it a short phrase or sentence that you can say in the time it takes to breathe in and out. My prayers start with a name for God and then my current need. In her book *Sacred Rhythms*, Ruth Haley Barton writes: "The breath prayer helps us pray when we don't know how to pray. It gives us a way to pray even when we can't pray formally."[5]

I'll give you an example of how I use this tool. Long, long ago there was a time when I had to buckle all four of my boys into the car. All four. This was before remote start on cars. And on hot Texas summer days, I would repeat, "Hurry! Get in your seats as fast as possible. We don't want to die!" (Sounds a bit dramatic unless you've experienced it.)

With so many kiddos, there was bound to be a protestor in the bunch. The one who arched his back, refusing to let me strap the five-point harness. After firmly pressing his little belly down and securing the buckles, I'd forcefully shut the car door. We hadn't even left the house and I was frustrated. As I walked from the passenger's side to the driver's side around the back of the car, I would pray a simple breath prayer: "Lord, give me peace." I'd slide behind the steering wheel, take a deep breath, and let the Spirit offer the peace I'd requested.

If you look throughout the Bible, you'll find examples of short prayers. Here are some of the ones I use based on Scripture:

- "Father, be my strength. Be with me. Hold me up." (Isa. 41:10)
- "Jesus, come quickly." (Rev. 22:20)
- "Spirit, bring life." (Rom. 8:2)
- "Lord, give me eyes to see how You see." (1 Sam. 16:7)
- "God, not my will but Yours be done." (Luke 22:42)
- "Jesus, I believe. Help my unbelief." (Mark 9:24)
- "Creator, remind me of my worth."(Ps. 139:13–16)
- "Spirit, guide and comfort me."(1 Cor. 2:7–13)

Often in our hardest mom moments, it isn't that we're bad moms. It's that we are limited human beings. And we frequently hit our limits (physical, spiritual, emotional). Inviting God to fill in the gaps isn't weak. It's an opportunity to deepen your intimacy with Him.

What if the mom had said no to Elijah when he'd asked for bread the first time? What if she didn't go to Elijah when her son stopped breathing? She would have missed out on two miracles: provision and resurrection. And most importantly, this Gentile woman wouldn't have encountered the One True God.

Just Enough

When I signed the contract for this book, I thought the topic would be different. Thankfully, before starting I asked God what He wanted me to write about, and He pointed me back to moms. When I asked Him for some sort of outline, He replied, "I'm gonna need you to rely on Me and other people in the same way you learned to lean on Me and others in your mothering."

About halfway into writing the book, I hit a bit of a roadblock. Thankfully, at the same time my long-time boy-mom mentor, Leslie

Johnson, reached out to have lunch. Using her life-coach training, she helped me figure out my initial whys of writing. She helped me see that sitting down one-on-one with each mom was impossible. But a book multiplied the message.

During a second life-coaching session, Leslie again asked thought-provoking questions about why I was stuck. One thing that rose to the surface was a lie that I needed chunks of uninterrupted time to write this book. I found that I was continually frustrated when distractions and commitments kept "stealing" my book-writing time. With a little more digging, we realized my method of producing the podcast didn't happen in chunks of time. In fact, my method of productivity didn't look like everyone else's. And that's okay.

God brought to mind the Israelites (yes, again). During their time in the wilderness, they were utterly dependent on God to meet their daily needs. He chose to feed them with little flakes of nourishment they gathered each day—manna. My new book-writing plan couldn't depend on large chunks of productive time. Instead, I needed to take note of the daily manna—the nuggets of wisdom, truth, and encouragement He wanted me to include.

In doing so, I thought of how this applies to our daily dependence on God in motherhood. How often we think if we don't have a three-hour quiet time then we shouldn't bother connecting with God. It was my mentor Leslie who gave me the idea to leave my Bible out on the counter. As I changed diapers, picked up toys, etc., I could read a verse to meditate on for the day.

We often desire to see big changes in our kids. To be confident that our mothering matters. What if we took a minute to notice the li'l flakes of goodness—the small moves in the right direction. That time he paused before throwing a car at his brother. The moment she reached out for your hand without you asking. A hug between siblings. A simple "I love you, Mommy." A gratitude list, of sorts.

When days are long and hard and no li'l flakes can be found, we can ask God, "Lord, what manna do You have for me today? Who do You say that I am? What morsel will You give to keep me going?"

The key with manna was the Israelites couldn't gather a bunch one day and store it up for the next couple days. If they tried to, it would spoil. Every day they depended on God. Every. Day. And the one day they didn't gather manna was on the Sabbath. In Jewish culture, Sabbath begins at sunset Friday night and ends at sunset Saturday night. A tradition created by God to remind His people they can "cease" for a day and trust Him to meet their needs. For those wandering Israelites, the manna gathered on Friday miraculously lasted until Sunday.

In 2017, I was invited on the trip of a lifetime to Israel. The Friday of our trip we ate lunch at the Jerusalem market. Rows and rows of booths sold their fresh veggies, spices, and meats. Energy pulsated through packed crowds gathering supplies for the next twenty-four hours as they were preparing for their weekly Friday night Shabbat dinner that kicks off Sabbath.

Our group was blessed to be invited into a local home for Shabbat dinner. A few things stood out to me: one was the extreme hospitality and the preparation and care in hosting twenty people with a multicourse meal. I also noted the inclusion of their children in the experience. They weren't told to "leave the adults alone." They wandered in and out of the room, witnessing the tradition and participating when able. And at one point during the meal, the father of the home said a blessing over each child and spoke a blessing over his wife.

My current small group at church has decided to adopt a version of this Jewish tradition. Once a month we gather in one of our homes for Shabbat dinner. During our time we intentionally call the kids together. We remind them how God created each of us uniquely and for His good purposes. Then the parents speak a blessing over each child. The hope is they will hold on to these words when the world tells them otherwise. And that they rest in who God made them to be instead of having to prove their worth through their work.

Maybe you're wondering why we are concerned with an Old Testament commandment to "remember the Sabbath day, to keep it holy" (Exod. 20:8 ESV). Doesn't the gospel set us free from the law?

Yes, after Jesus's death and resurrection, keeping the law was not required to be right with God. Christ perfectly fulfilled the law. But keeping the law is for our benefit. Jesus Himself said, "The Sabbath was made for man, not man for the Sabbath" (Mark 2:27). God rested after creation. Jesus rested during His ministry. Maybe like our kids at Shabbat dinner, you need a reminder that your worth/value isn't based on what you do but on who God is.

If you have nothing left to give, have you considered resting? Maybe you know you need rest, but you haven't considered the *kind* of rest you need. In 2018, Dr. Saundra Dalton-Smith came on my podcast and shared the seven types of rest she discovered after her own meltdown. The types she mentioned are physical, mental, spiritual, emotional, social, sensory, and creative. She shared simple ways to add rest into our lives. Often, it's not that a mom *can't* rest, it's that she doesn't let herself.

> Rest is about restoration. It keeps me in that place where when woundings come, if I want to be restored, I have to allow myself to get to a place where I lay down my ability to try to fix it. I don't have the power to fix it. He only has the power to fix every one of the seven types. And rest is where God is coming in some type of either spiritual or physical or scientific way that's healing us.[6]

Sabbath is good for me. It doesn't have to look like the traditional Jewish experience. I may choose to "cease" from checking social media for twenty-four hours. The key is to choose what will help *you* set apart that day or a certain period of time from the other days.

58

Here's what else Sabbath reminds me of: the world doesn't end when I stop striving. My work doesn't make me worthy. That weekly reminder keeps my heart in the right position as I continue to serve and pour out.

You have every right to feel weary. You are a limited human being. But I want to remind you (so you don't have to learn the hard way) that God is available. He offers His limitless love. His presence and power are as close as your breath. And His soul restoring can be found in intentional rest.

Isolating Idea
I have nothing left to give.

Connecting Truth
I am a limited human being, dependent on a limitless God.

Discussion Questions

1. Do you currently have a time in your day to remind yourself of God's never-ending source of love? If you don't currently have a time, brainstorm with your group when you could try adding a five-minute habit of remembering.

2. When have others been used by God to provide what you need right when you needed it?

3. What are some breath prayers that could help get you through your weary moments?

4. What's a way you could collect "manna" moments in your day? A note in your phone, a journal on the counter, sticky notes? Brainstorm ideas on how to notice the gifts of provision in each day.

5. Take Dr. Dalton-Smith's rest quiz (www.restquiz.com). Discuss which types of rest you need and brainstorm how you could get them. Have you considered "ceasing" from something to rest?

four

Seeing Is Believing

Being at the park with my little kids, there are lots of people there but no one talking to me. It's hard when you feel lonely surrounded by people.

—Kathryn

Middle schoolers huddled in a circle. I stood just outside the group, peering in, longing to hear what was shared. As a homeschooled eighth grader, it was obvious I didn't belong. And the longer I stood among them, but not with them, the heavier the loneliness weighed.

And then Jesus beckoned me to follow. To walk out of the room and outside. We stood facing a small familiar pond, edged with cattails. He directed my attention to an odd, corndog-shaped plant.

"I take great delight in my creation. What may look useless to some, brings Me great joy. I created you, Heather, and I take great delight in you. When you feel awkward and unimportant, remember the cattail. See yourself the way I see you, crowned with beauty."

No, Jesus didn't actually take me to a pond. But in a season when that middle-school self was breaking into my adult social life, I asked Jesus to help.

As a forty-year-old mom, I still felt like an outsider peering over backs, longing to be invited into the circle. I believed the lie that I was "too weird" or "not worthy of other people's attention." And God graciously healed my skewed identity by transforming an actual painful memory of indifference. He drew me to Himself. Away from the crowd, the in-crowd, to a peaceful pond. Then He reminded me of who I am and Whose I am. As the Creator, He has the authority to label His creation "lovely." In choosing solitude with God, I aligned my heart with His so that I'm not pulled to less-satisfying sources of identity and worth.

Perhaps you get it. You've stood on the outside of a circle, longing to be invited and included. Disappointed that you remain unseen and unacknowledged. Your middle-school self begins to speak up with words of "too much" or "not enough."

"Loneliness is the subjective feeling that you're lacking the social connections you need," says Dr. Vivek Murthy. "It can feel like being stranded, abandoned, or cut off from the people with whom you belong—even if you're surrounded by other people. What's missing when you're lonely is the feeling of closeness, trust, and the affection of genuine friends, loved ones, and community."[1]

Motherhood can disconnect us from the movement of society or a career path or prior friendships. We can be surrounded by people and feel alone. Untethered from who we were before having a baby. Or stranded by the seclusion of having multiple young children. Perhaps a stain in your story keeps you from "fitting in" or even led to rejection from your community. If you feel like an outsider, you are not alone.

Seen by God

The idea of feeling like an outsider reminds me of a story in the book of Genesis. God promised Abram that Abram would be the father of many and be given a land and that the whole world would be blessed through him. But he remained childless. And he questioned God, saying, "What will you give me, for I continue childless?" and "Behold, you have given me no offspring" (Gen. 15:2–3 ESV). God reinforced the promise with a covenant after directing Abram's gaze to the stars and saying, "So shall your offspring be" (v. 5 ESV).

His wife, Sarai, listening to the voice of unbelief rather than to the Lord, impatiently came up with a plan: "Behold now, the Lord has prevented me from bearing children. Go in to my servant; it may be that I shall obtain children by her" (Gen. 16:2 ESV). Abram chose to listen to his wife's voice and forgot the promise of God. When Hagar became pregnant, Sarai began to despise her. "Then Sarai dealt harshly with her, and she fled from her" (v. 6 ESV). Hagar fled to the wilderness. The angel of the Lord found her and began a conversation with her.

Have you ever wondered who "the angel of the Lord" is? I did a little research for us. This "being" interacts with humanity throughout the Old Testament and speaks on behalf of Yahweh (aka, God) and *as* Yahweh. The complex, yet consistent, pattern of distinguishing this figure is important. There is a New Testament figure who speaks for God and is God. Have you figured it out yet? Some scholars believe these Old Testament references are appearances by Jesus before His immaculate conception.

Here we have a pregnant slave, discarded by her master, alone in the wilderness, and preincarnate Jesus greets her by name and by her identity. I remember what it felt like to be vulnerably pregnant. But I was never truly alone, cast out, or mistreated. Hagar was. And Jesus not only came near but knew her intimately—her name and her identity.

Then He questioned her in verse 8. "Where have you come from, and where are you going?" She told Him she was fleeing her master. He instructed her to return and blessed her with the promise that her offspring would be many—a glimpse of hope.

In response, Hagar used the name for God not used up to this point in the Bible: "You are a God of seeing. . . . Truly here I have seen him who looks after me" (Gen. 16:13 ESV).

Since God's character is unchanging, He remains the God who sees and looks after us today. He sees you. He sees your child. Like my friend Sara Hagerty said, "God's eyes are the only ones that have the right and perfect evaluation of any given moment, and His opinion is the only one that matters. We can ask Him, 'What are you thinking about me right now?'"[2] But how do we do that?

This Same Jesus

Have you ever considered that, like Hagar, you could meet with Jesus today? That His appearances weren't just for biblical characters? Jesus met, healed, and taught hundreds of people before His crucifixion. After He rose from the dead and before ascending to heaven, Jesus made appearances to over five hundred people.

During His ascension to heaven, while the disciples were looking at the sky, two heavenly beings said to them, "Men of Galilee, why do you stand here looking into the sky? *This same Jesus*, who has been taken from you into heaven, will come back in the same way you have seen him go into heaven" (Acts 1:11, emphasis added).

Scholars agree this is a prophecy of the second advent, Christ's return, which has not yet happened. But does Jesus appear to believers today? After He ascended to heaven, will He stay silent until His triumphant return?

I don't believe so.

Two examples come to my mind. One is with Stephen, after he had given testimony about the truth of Jesus and before he was stoned to death. "But he, full of the Holy Spirit, gazed into heaven and saw the glory of God, and Jesus standing at the right hand of God. And he said, 'Behold, I see the heavens opened, and the Son of Man standing at the right hand of God'" (Acts 7:55–56 ESV). The key here is how Stephen became aware of Jesus's presence in a moment of suffering: *while* filled with the Holy Spirit.

Another appearance was to Saul on the road to Damascus. "Now as he went on his way, he approached Damascus, and suddenly a light from heaven shone around him. And falling to the ground, he heard a voice saying to him, 'Saul, Saul, why are you persecuting me?' And he said, 'Who are you, Lord?' And he said, 'I am Jesus, whom you are persecuting. But rise and enter the city, and you will be told what you are to do'" (Acts 9:3–6 ESV).

The Scripture is clear that Jesus appeared to Saul and was speaking from heaven. But what I find interesting is the fact that Jesus was interacting with those on earth. He was not distant and removed.

Growing up I was taught that these stories in Acts happened for the establishment of the church. But then once established, the Holy Spirit didn't work the same way. I knew a lot about the Holy Spirit but didn't believe I would see the same power in my life because "God doesn't work that way anymore."

I operated out of those beliefs for years, until I read Francis Chan's book *Forgotten God* with a group of spiritual mentors/ friends.[3] During the summer we met early in the morning once a week to discuss the book. One morning I felt the need to ask a hard question: "I know that the Holy Spirit is the Third Person of the Trinity. That we are promised to be filled with the Spirit when we profess faith in Jesus. And through the Spirit we are given power to do the things God instructs us to do." Then a big, empty pause. "But I just don't see that kind of power in my life. I don't see God moving in big ways or the 'fruit' of 'love, joy, kindness,' etc. Why is that?"

The three ladies sitting there looked at each other like they had a secret—an answer they were unsure should be shared with me.

Finally one of them said, "Do you really want to know?" To which I responded, "Um, of course! That's why I asked the question."

Two of them invited me to join them in prayer to ask God to show me why I wasn't experiencing the power of the Holy Spirit in my life. He graciously revealed my belief that "God just doesn't work that way anymore." So I simply prayed out loud, "God, forgive me. I have wrongly believed that Your Spirit is no longer working in this world." The gals then prompted me not only to ask for forgiveness but to accept the forgiveness He generously offers.

This is where it got a bit weird for me (and may be hard for you to believe). My forearms started getting warm. With my eyes closed, it felt like the room started to spin. I'm not even kidding. Definitely not your typical book club meeting.

But then again, why would I expect God to work one way in the Bible and differently hundreds of years later in my life? Look at when the promised Holy Spirit arrived to the first followers of Jesus. "And suddenly there came from heaven a sound like a mighty rushing wind, and it filled the entire house where they were sitting. And divided tongues as of fire appeared to them and rested on each one of them. And they were filled with the Holy Spirit" (Acts 2:2–4 ESV).

That time of prayer (confession and forgiveness) left a dramatic mark on my story. There is a "before" that moment and an "after." A new level of intimacy with God that had lain dormant for all my years following Jesus. Like I had been following from a distance instead of walking hand-in-hand. The Samaritan woman disqualified herself from "living water" because of her past. I disqualified myself from access to God's infinite power by holding a wrong belief.

The realignment of my belief system is what Romans 8 refers to with the phrase "set the mind." The original Greek word is *phronema*, which "connects how the individual processes opinion-making to how they act."[4] Aligning my thought processes with the

Spirit impacts how I interact with others. Romans 8:6 promises, "For to set the mind on the flesh is death, but to set the mind on the Spirit is life and peace" (ESV). Life and peace to my parenting. Life and peace to my friendships. Life and peace to my ministry. Life and peace.

Jesus knew that when He left, a Helper and Comforter would come. "But the Helper, the Holy Spirit, whom the Father will send in my name, he will teach you all things and bring to your remembrance all that I have said to you" (John 14:26 ESV). Like Stephen, who was "filled with the Holy Spirit" when he saw Jesus, we, as believers filled with the Holy Spirit, are invited to meet with Jesus through prayer. He longs to meet with us. A primary role of the Holy Spirit is to point us back to Jesus, to remind us of all He has said.

What I'm suggesting is that you pause long enough to let the Spirit impress on your heart what He longs for you to know. I have never heard an audible voice. In a quiet moment I pause, acknowledge God's presence, and ask Him to speak (using a variation of Samuel's prayer from 1 Samuel 3:10, "Speak, Lord, your servant is listening"). Then I pay attention to the thoughts that cross my mind. If a thought lines up with Scripture, builds up, encourages, even convicts, then I interpret that to be from the Lord.

The most common criticism of this practice is, "How do you know it's not just your own thoughts?" I go back to that list. If I hear, "You are an idiot. You will never have friends. You are a terrible mom. Do you really think God loves you?" I can guarantee that's not from God. It may be my own thoughts, and it could be the enemy trying to discourage, deceive, or distract me (like he did to Eve in the garden in Genesis 3:1: "Did God really say . . . ?"). But if I've been in God's Word and the Holy Spirit prompts me to remember truth I've previously read, why wouldn't I attribute those thoughts to God? His Word brought to mind by His Spirit.

My friend Kelsey Phillips came on the show to talk about her experience listening to the Lord. She reminded me how, in the Old Testament, God spoke through burning bushes and donkeys. Although she hasn't experienced either one, He has spoken to her through Scripture and through an internal thinking voice. "He does speak to me in pictures, and sometimes He'll just give me a word that'll just flash across my mind. But my husband, when he gets in his time with the Lord, the Lord really gives him a sensation of peace or knowing. There's a physicalness to my husband's hearing from the Lord."[5]

Kelsey suggests spending time with God and asking "friendship questions." Ask God these questions and then write down any impressions, thoughts, words, or pictures that come to mind:

- What do You see when You look at me?
- Am I carrying anything I shouldn't be?
- Do You have a word or a picture for me to hold on to in this season?

Kelsey shared how taking time to meet with Jesus and listening through prayer has changed her parenting: "I operate out of a place of more wholeness than brokenness. We will never be fully whole until we're in heaven. But as Jesus heals wounds, when people hurt my feelings, I can go to Him and He can walk me through what was going on and give me the peace to forgive, or He can just speak affirmation to me. There's a shift when my identity is realigned with Him. And I know who I am and Whose I am. My parenting is so much kinder and gentler and easier."[6]

Perhaps you are drawn to having an intimate friendship with Jesus through the Holy Spirit. But something inside still taunts you as unworthy. Too far gone to meet with God. Too many mistakes to be really seen and known by your Creator. I'd like to offer you a story to convince you those are lies.

Never Too Messy

Sitting in my favorite leather chair, with three boys off to school and one still asleep, I enjoyed a rare quiet, late morning. That is until I heard little footsteps on the stairs and a jumbled mix of words like: "poop," "mess," "yucky."

Coming from my calm "reminded I'm in the river of love" place, I entered his bedroom to find poop footprints. Poop. Footprints.

I followed the tracks into the bathroom and saw a pile of toilet paper overflowing from the toilet. Then my eye caught the pile in front of the toilet, a mix of poo and paper. Lying nearby was a set of discarded footed pjs covered in . . . you guessed it . . . poop.

I glanced back at my son to see a horrified expression on his face. A mix of shame and guilt. Honestly, if this scenario had happened on a morning we had to rush to go somewhere or all the boys were home, I may have responded with anger or annoyance. Thankfully, because of my extended quiet morning and no need to rush, I graciously offered him help and comfort. "It's gonna be okay, buddy. We can totally clean this mess up. Why don't you get in the bath?" An invitation he adamantly refused. He wouldn't even step foot into the bathroom. As I coaxed him in, the closer he got to the mess, the more upset he became.

I finally calmed him down and settled him into a warm bath. While he soaked, I got on my knees to gather up the poo-covered toilet paper in plastic grocery bags. That's when I felt his sweet hand rubbing my back as he gently said, "Thank you, Mommy. I love you so much." (Cue tears.)

In that moment all I could think was, "I could have missed this." If I had responded with frustration, I wouldn't have received kindness in return. The same measure of grace and care I offered, he extended.

Let's imagine what would have happened if he'd never told me about the mess? If my son had let shame keep me from cleaning up his mess? If he had continued to push me away and deny its existence because of his embarrassment by its presence? The mess wouldn't have gone away. The stench would have caught up with him eventually. And he would not have the feeling of love from his mom.

How often do we do the same with God? Keeping our dirtiest, worst actions hidden from Him . . . as if He can't already see into our hearts. We often stiff-arm Him and continue, like Adam and Eve in the garden, to separate ourselves in shame. We feel unworthy to walk in His presence. Like my son, we believe the mess is too much to clean up. We forget how much He loves us.

We forget that no one is too far gone, no mess is too much for Him. Nothing about us will ever change His love for us. And when He sees you, He sees the perfection of His son. What are you trying to cover up with piles of toilet paper? What areas of your soul are you too ashamed to reveal? Start with a simple prayer: "God, I know nothing is hidden from You. Remove the shame." And tell Him what you believe is too much for Him.

Then ask yourself, "What have I been believing?" Maybe something you've believed about God (e.g., "God is angry with me"). Or something you've believed about others (e.g., "People cannot be trusted"). Perhaps a wrong belief about yourself (e.g., "I don't deserve attention and care from other people").

A key step in freedom from the thing you've been hiding is to align with God. Adjust how you've been thinking about it with how He feels. This process starts with confession. Not the kind of "beat myself up" or "woe is me" confession. But like the confession I shared earlier of how I wasn't believing rightly about the Holy Spirit. Simply stating your wrong belief back to God.

Something like, "Lord, forgive me. I have been believing that I can meet everyone's needs. That their happiness and approval are based on my performance. I know You tell us that if we confess, You are faithful and just to forgive us and cleanse us. Help me release control to You."

Then receive His forgiveness and freedom. Let it pour over you. Verbalize accepting it. "Lord, I receive Your forgiveness."

Free to Welcome

Have you ever been so consumed with your own identity crisis that you were unable to see the pain and needs of others? To even connect with your kids? Many times, I've been overly occupied with my wounds and blind to the wounds of others. But through meeting with Jesus in prayer, like Kelsey suggested, the hard parts of my past have been healed. Like the story I shared at the start of this chapter, Jesus reframed the memory of being ignored and feeling unimportant. He healed a wound of perceived rejection so I could move forward in freedom to be hospitable to others. When I truly grasped how God saw me (adored, beautiful, accepted), I was free to see those around me. To extend an invitation to them to be seen by God.

My friend Kate is an "includer" and loyal listener of my podcast. One day on a walk around her neighborhood, she saw a mom across the street pushing a stroller. Not only did she see her, she could hear that the mom was listening to the *Don't Mom Alone* podcast. With more bravery than I have, she crossed the street and invited that mom to join her podcast club. She saw her. She invited her. And I'm confident that in their gatherings together, she will give her hope only a mom a bit further along the journey can offer.

Kate understood these words from the apostle Paul to the church of Thessalonica: "So speak encouraging words to one another. Build up hope so you'll all be together in this, no one left out, no one left behind" (1 Thess. 5:11 MSG). In the middle of trials, the end is blurry and distant. We need one another to *build up hope*. That building comes when we seek out someone who has been there and survived.

At the beginning of 2020, I took a break from work and took a walk around my neighborhood (before the pandemic made it the popular thing to do). As I was heading home, I saw a mom pushing a stroller in front of my house. But unlike Kate, I didn't say anything. No head nod or subtle wave. Earbuds in, I walked straight up my front steps.

As the founder of a mom ministry, you'd think I'd have been bold enough to introduce myself, tell her about my podcast, or *something*. Instead, I made my way to the door, turned the key, and let myself inside. I "saw" the new mom pushing the stroller, but my engagement ended there.

Fast-forward a couple months to March 2020, the start of quarantine. I was pretty geared up to finally work on some decluttering projects. One area of need was my growing pile of books sent to me by publishers. I'm honored that authors want to come on the show. And blessed by the gift of not only one book, but often two or three copies of the same book.

The spring weather was ideal for daily (sometimes twice daily) neighborhood walks. I noticed so many more of our neighbors out and about. Given the increase in foot traffic, I decided to create a book giveaway in our front yard. It was a win-win. Decluttering meets ministry. I filled up a couple plastic bins with these fantastic books and left them out front. Each night I dragged the bins back inside to protect the books from any pop-up storms.

Around the same time, our church decided to print yard signs that read, "How can we pray for you?" For a few weeks I had sticky notes attached and a pen hanging off the sign for folks walking by to write a request. We had a few neighbors vulnerably share fears or desires. Then we started noticing that the notes would blow off and we were probably littering more than helping. That's when I pulled out the Sharpie and wrote, "DM me on Instagram @DontMomAlone."

My thought was not only connecting with neighbors but possibly pointing them to the podcast for encouragement and support. What actually happened was these neighborhood moms encouraged me.

One day I vulnerably shared on Instagram. A city official had just announced an extension to the quarantine. It felt like I was nearing the end of a 5K and someone told me it was actually a marathon. I wrote, "I ended the day crying in the shower. If you got to the end of yourself this week, you're not alone." There was a part of me that wanted to give a spiritual answer to my sorrow. I also felt the need to quickly prove I wasn't a complete mess. When friends called to comfort me, I responded with, "Oh, it's not that bad." Lastly, I struggled to accept the help offered to me. Especially when a single mom friend, who lost her job during the quarantine, had my favorite coffee delivered. Shouldn't I be helping her instead of the other way around?

But admitting my real situation allowed sixty-three moms to connect with me. Through direct messages they sent me encouragement ("Praying for you right now"), gratitude ("Thank you for being real"), and identification ("This was me last week. I felt the crushing feeling of everything going on").

That afternoon I opened our door to find a little clothes hanger made out of a pipe cleaner. A "shirt" hanging on it made out of a sticky note and the words, "Hang in there. —Your neighbor across the street." The next day a handwritten note in my mailbox with some skin care samples and a mom's phone number. "You aren't alone. Call anytime."

Days later I saw that mom walk by our house. She had one daughter in her arms while pulling a red wagon that held a screaming little girl. Later that morning I went for a walk. When I passed her house, I texted the phone number she'd given me. "Walking by your house right now. Praying for you." She texted back, "Thank you. We need it. It's been a hard day."

I know. I see you, Mama. More importantly, God sees you.

Isolating Idea

I am an outsider.

Connecting Truth

I am seen, valued, and free to welcome others.

Discussion Questions

1. Share about a time when you were or felt like you were alone in the wilderness. How did God help you feel seen and known?

2. Have you ever spent time sitting with Jesus and asking Him how He sees you?

3. Is there a part of your story that holds you back from connecting with others? Can you make the time this week to bring it to God? To align your heart with His and let Him heal your story?

4. Have you ever considered "seeing" those around you instead of just passing by? Why do you think you don't engage those around you?

5. Are there moms in your community you've seen but have been hesitant to connect with? In what creative way can you reach out and start that relationship?

SECTION TWO

Supported
by Others

five

No Mom Is an Island

The way I experience isolation is by not letting people in my home for fear they would see the "real" me and not want to be my friend anymore. Fearing that I would put too much stress on others and be too much for them, I just kept to myself. Isolation for me was just cutting everyone else out and not wanting to place my burdens on anyone.

—Samantha

Panicked, I gripped the door handle and considered jumping out of the car. My body filled with adrenaline. And my mind was not even close to catching up with the wave of fear.

I had to get out. And get away.

But from what?

No one was chasing me.

My husband was driving. My four young boys were strapped in car seats in the back of our Suburban. We were simply buying lunch from a fried-chicken restaurant drive-through. (And no, it wasn't Chick-fil-A, because this anxiety attack chose to arrive on Sunday, after church.)

Reflecting back on that moment, on top of the shame, I have to fight feeling guilty.

Isn't it wrong for a Christian woman with four healthy children, a loving husband, a great home, financial security, and "everything going for her" to feel that level of stress and fear? I *should* be able to handle this beautiful life I've been given. Sure, everyone has hard days. But "good Christians" don't let overwhelming moments take them down. Right?

Those were my inner thoughts.

And yet, if *you* reached out to me on a hard day, feeling anxious, I would never layer guilt on your weary soul, telling you how you *should* feel. Or that you must not have enough faith.

So why do I talk to myself that way? How did I get here? I had good friends, mentors, and a loving spouse. A solid support network. Untapped.

At that point I never considered sharing negative emotions with friends. My goal was to keep up an image that I've got it all together, especially since I was writing a blog called *God Centered Mom*. Because a "God Centered Mom" doesn't have anxiety. And she definitely doesn't want to jump out of a car in the fried-chicken drive-through . . . after church no less!

It didn't matter if I called it an "anxiety attack" or a "breakdown." What mattered is I could no longer continue without community. I could no longer carry my thoughts, fears, and worries alone. So, at my husband's urging, I texted a friend. A friend who understood these thoughts and feelings. I simply asked for her counselor's phone number.

Vulnerable with Safe People

For the next month I held on to the number but never called. Convincing myself I felt better already. Falsely thinking perhaps I didn't need to see a counselor after all. Thankfully, during that month of feeling better, I started to share my story with safe friends, letting them know things weren't right.

If you're wondering who you can consider "safe," author Shauna Niequist shared an idea on how to figure it out:

> Start small. Go to coffee with someone and gauge their willingness to be vulnerable with you. If you want people to be vulnerable with you, then you have to go first. You take the risk of saying, "One thing that's been hard for me this week is . . ." You wade in with some of the truth from your life. If they respond with, "Oh my gosh, I don't have that same issue, but I totally get it cuz I have . . ." If they meet you there, then you keep going. But if they respond with, "Oh my gosh this latte is so good." Loud and clear. I hear you. You have given me the signal that you don't want to have that kind of relationship with me. That's totally fine. I have had that happen to me a million times.[1]

Surprisingly the more safe people I told, the easier it became to tell. To say, "You know, after each of my babies I felt overwhelmed, anxious, and sad. Perhaps I've had some form of undiagnosed postpartum depression each time." I was amazed how many responded, "Yes, I know those feelings." And "Yes, you should speak with someone." And "Talking is healing. Keep talking."

After exchanging stories with one friend, the term "depression" didn't seem like the right label for me. I know I'm not supposed to compare. But she had suffered deep pain in her season of depression. A time when she could barely get out of bed and struggled to have energy to feed her kids. In my case, I didn't feel like calling friends back or planting fall flowers. My version didn't seem extreme enough to count. Maybe what I felt wasn't depression after all. She quickly set me straight. "Heather, I don't think what you are experiencing needs a label. You just don't feel like yourself. That's enough." Her permission to acknowledge the reality of how I felt let me move forward and address it.

Because *the Heather I know* threw fun New Year's Eve parties in her house with a live band while kids slept soundly upstairs. *The Heather I know* laughs loud and dances freely. *The Heather I know* gives of herself without holding back. *The Heather I know* answers the phone on the first ring, eager to encourage the woman on the other end. *The Heather I know* creates and enjoys beauty. *The Heather I know* doesn't want to miss a thing. And I missed her.

So I made the phone call and boldly scheduled my first counseling session. Because I want to love the Lord my God with *all* my mind. *All* my heart. *All* my strength. Like Pastor John Mark Comer says, "Emotional health isn't just about me feeling better. The whole thing is about love. You can't be emotionally unhealthy and loving to the degree that you want. The degree that you are emotionally healthy is the degree to which you have capacity to love. It's the greatest apologetic for emotional health."[2]

When I entered the counselor's office, I discovered that the cliché is true. I commented on the couch and loved when she replied, "Don't worry, I won't make you lie down on it." She loved God. She studied at seminary. She didn't want to blame parents (remember, they are only 30 percent responsible). But she said life words like "You have come a long way, but you have some baggage to set down. I'll help you do that."

Getting professional help, taking medication, and receiving other treatments are wise ways to heal the imbalance caused by pregnancy. They are tools to get you to a healthy place. The verse "Preparing your minds for action" (1 Pet. 1:13 ESV) encouraged me to get better. The Greek for "prepare" means to "gather up what entangles you." By taking care of what trips me up, I can be ready for action, putting down baggage so I'm ready to serve Him. Honestly, meeting with the counselor was just the beginning of the untangling. Because one of the gifts of motherhood is dealing with all your junk that comes to the surface. Then inviting others into your mess and together getting curious about your reactive responses to life circumstances. Asking each other questions like,

Why do you respond the way you do? What is behind your thought process? How can you get the help you need to respond differently?

Shauna Niequist also recommended starting with a small group of people you are investing in long term. Make a plan to deepen relationships. Pick two to three people and meet with them once a week for a year. "When somebody tells the truth about their life, especially the ugly side, the scary side, it sets you free to do the same. It invites you to live with that same vulnerability and courage. We're all so similar. We're scared by the same things. If you don't say it out loud, you start to think there is something wrong with you. But you're not crazy. You're not alone."[3]

I can testify that what she suggests works. A few years ago, after finishing the Celebrate Recovery study, my small group at church transitioned to a processing group. We started off formally, with two trained leaders who at the beginning of each session read guidelines to keep communication lines open.

In Dr. John Townsend's book *Boundaries*, he sets up some helpful guidelines for fostering a safe group discussion:

- Be emotionally present. Speak from your heart, rather than from your opinions or head.
- Speak in the first person. Say "I feel," rather than "people feel."
- Allow periods of silence. Though it may be somewhat uncomfortable at first, silence can allow people to reflect deeper on how they are feeling, it can lead to a transition to a new topic, or it can allow people to simply listen to God.
- Don't fix or give advice, just *be there* for others. We often "advise" each other to avoid looking at our own issues. Attune to their feelings and thoughts by sharing what they must be feeling (e.g., "I can see how sad that is for you").[4]

After someone shares, we give space and ask them what they need from the group. Whether they need to be heard, supported, given input, or provided direction. Through this process I've learned to listen more than offer advice. To ask for what's needed before rushing in with what I think they need. And give space for my mom friend to process through her emotions to get to those repeating internal mental tapes. Once she says out loud the thing that has been torturing her, we can examine it together. Hold it up against the truth of God's Word (if that's what she asks to do). And connect with the shared experience of being vulnerable together.

Pushing past fear of rejection and my insecurities has been worth it more than it hasn't. Community can be used by God to provide the help I need in times of trouble. Like Solomon wisely instructed, "Two are better than one, because they have a good return for their labor: If either of them falls down, one can help the other up. But pity anyone who falls and has no one to help them up" (Eccles. 4:9–10).

A Step Ahead

One night.

I had only spent one night at home with my first son. He'd slept like a baby (translation: he was up every couple hours to eat). After thirty minutes feeding him and then changing his diaper, I spent another forty-five minutes trying to get him to fall back asleep. Repeat. All. Night. Long.

My heart sank as morning light shone into his nursery and I started the feed-change-sleep cycle once again. Is this the rest of my life? Will every night for the rest of my life require complete sacrifice of comfort?

Sitting in shock at my realization, I heard a soft knock at the door. "It's Mom. I have breakfast for you. Is it okay to bring it in?"

My voice squeaked out, "Yes, please."

As she set the tray in front of me, a tear slid down my cheek. A mix of gratitude, exhaustion, and hope. Her presence reminded me that mothering a newborn isn't forever. But being a mom is. Have I ever really noticed the sacrifices my mom made for me?

She had a sixteen-year-old and an eleven-year-old when I showed up on the scene. Instead of continuing to pursue a traditional teaching career, she stayed home to educate me and my younger brother. She made her own pasta, was part of a vegetable co-op, and bought chemical-free plastic wrap. Not that those things are a part of the "good mom" formula, just hallmarks of my childhood and her intention to do the best she could do.

All these years later, once again she showed up. This time as a mother serving her weary, new-mom daughter. But she delivered more than breakfast. She brought perspective and wisdom as I entered unknown territory. Guidance was available if I simply humbled myself or became desperate enough to ask for advice. Which, unfortunately, I do not take advantage of as often as I could.

While blessed by a fantastic mom, she didn't live in the same city (or at times even the same country). Thankfully the church we chose highly values mentorship. One of our church icons, Vickie Kraft, a mom of five children, attended seminary in her fifties. Not only did she serve as our first minister to women, she cofounded the Titus 2:4 mentoring ministry and authored several books, including *Women Mentoring Women*. Her influence is still felt today. Those mentored by her are now mentoring me and others.

For example, it was during the church women's retreat that I met Miss Nancy. Even though we were both living in Dallas, she used to live in Indiana. In fact, for years she was in a Bible study taught by my mom! #SmallWorld. Being new to Texas, having a connection with someone who knew my family gave me such comfort. It didn't stop there. Nancy mentored Leslie, a mom of four boys. Fast-forward ten years, when I picked up my third son from the nursery, Leslie was one of the nursery volunteers. She had picked up on the fact that I had three small boys. One week she kindly extended an invitation. "I don't know if you are in-terested, but I'm starting a MomHeart group. We'll meet in the evening every other week. I'd love for you to join us." As a weary mom (see chapter 3), I jumped at the chance to be poured into by a woman a little further down the road. As you've already read in this book, Leslie has been a bountiful source of wisdom and perspective in my life.

I know our church is unique. And not everyone is blessed with so many mentors at their disposal. For years I have told moms that mentors don't usually knock on your door and offer to mentor you. But I just had coffee with a friend, and she told me about her mentor, Susan. When I asked how she started that relationship, my friend literally said, "Well, she is my neighbor. When we moved into the neighborhood, she knocked on my door and introduced herself. We've met at least once a month for years."

The reality is most likely a mentor (or mentee) won't come knocking on your door. Leslie says she asks both ways. She asked Miss Nancy to meet with her. And Leslie often extends invitations to have coffee, lunch, or a walk with younger moms.

If you would like to initiate a mentor relationship, I have some tips to get you started. First, consider what area of your life needs mentoring. Discipline? Marriage? Work/life balance? Home man-agement? Once you identify what you need to be mentored in, look around for anyone in your community who is one step ahead of you in that area. Not necessarily one step ahead in a season of life, but someone who can guide you. Pray for God to open your eyes to see that person. (I'm not saying that flippantly . . . there is power in asking God for community.) Then make your request. Realize you aren't asking to meet together every week for the rest of your life. You don't want to intimidate and overwhelm this person. Simply ask if she could meet with you *one time*—for coffee, lunch, at the park while the kids play.

When you get together, determine if you feel like she is a good match for you. Did you leave the conversation encouraged and inspired? That's a good sign. (Leslie said her husband always commented on how happy she was on days she met with Miss Nancy.) Ask if she would be interested in continuing to meet once or twice a month. Communicate your expectations. If you are the mentor, determine if perhaps the mom may be better served by a professional counselor.

Make the mentoring relationship work for you. Have the times to meet fit into something you're already doing. I remember Leslie coming over to my house. We sat on the back porch and chatted while the boys ran around the backyard and played. In fact, having her witness some of my struggles was super helpful. I could invite her advice on issues in real time instead of trying to remember the ways I was struggling to parent. Maybe you ask your mentor/mentee to join you on a walk. I had a younger mom invite me to meet up at her house. I brought my dog, and she pushed her youngest daughter in a stroller while our other kids were in school. During your time together you could simply ask two questions: What are you learning from the Lord? What specifically can I pray about for you? Listen. Pray right there.

She Needs You

I don't remember what holiday it was. I know it wasn't important enough for my husband to take off work, but the kids were out of school. The boys and I were hanging out at home when my phone rang. I answered and heard her crying. She simply asked, "Can I come over?"

When I opened the door, I saw my friend and her husband. He held her hand, looked at me, and said, "She needs you." Then his head dropped in shame, and he admitted he had returned to an affair. Overcome by the Holy Spirit, I reached out and took both of their hands and said, "This does not have to end in divorce. I've known many couples with infidelity in their story who have found healing. The story of God's love is persistent in the face of our continual unfaithfulness. If you want to restore your relationship, God will walk alongside you and embolden your way."

In that moment my friend and her husband needed to know they weren't the only ones who've experienced this particular pain. They needed me to build up hope.

Have you ever had a friend reach out to you in a hard season and you didn't know how to help? You felt ill-equipped with what to do or what to say. Maybe you tried to be supportive and did more damage than good.

How do we help without hurting?

A few years ago I attended a yearlong course learning biblically based prayer tools. The goal of the class was to equip us to help others through prayer. Part of our training was learning about our identity as children of God and the authority we hold in the spiritual realm.

In the unseen, spiritual world, God has the last say—the ultimate authority over any other spiritual being. The Greek word for "authority" is *exousia*, and it is used 103 times in the New Testament. The *New Bible Dictionary* defines it as "rightful, actual, and unimpeded power to act, or to possess, control, use or dispose of, something or somebody."[5]

Because of Jesus's work on the cross, we are grafted into the family of God, coheirs with Christ. Like it says in John 1:12, "To all who did receive [Christ], to those who believed in his name, he gave the right [authority—*exousia*] to become children of God." We are given authority and identity to do God's work on this earth. To bring the kingdom of heaven here.

"For our struggle is not against flesh and blood, but against the rulers, against the authorities, against the powers of this dark world and against the spiritual forces of evil in the heavenly realms" (Eph. 6:12). If there is a spiritual battle, will God leave us defenseless? Absolutely not! We have a role in the battle, and He equips with the power and authority of the Holy Spirit.

When Jesus walked this earth, He ministered to others. He also invited the disciples to join Him. He said, "Whoever believes in

86

me will also do the works that I do; and greater works than these will he do, because I'm going to the Father. . . . And I will ask the Father, and he will give you another Helper, to be with you forever" (John 14:12, 16 ESV).

With the help of the Holy Spirit, you can "put on the full armor of God, so that you can take your stand against the devil's schemes" (Eph. 6:11). But what does that look like in our everyday moments?

Imagine you are having coffee with a friend. She shares that she is worried about whether her son's behavior is normal. Should she seek professional help, or will he grow out of it? Of course you will listen as she shares. Maybe you'll ask how she feels and what she needs from you. Then like a lot of us do, you may offer an "I'll pray for you," but you never do.

What if before you parted ways, you asked if you could pray a blessing over her? Not just praying to God about her situation (often termed "intercessory prayer"). But listening to God for her and then praying a blessing over her from what you hear. Right there in the coffee shop (or living room with little ones running around).

There are a couple forms of blessing prayer that I have learned. One is to bless someone with Scripture that God brings to mind. For example, if someone is anxious, you can pray a blessing of Psalm 23: "The Lord is your Good Shepherd. He restores your soul." Or pray a reminder that Jesus's yoke is easy and light (Matt. 11:30).

The second form of blessing prayer is to pray in the opposite spirit. If the person is battling shame, pray a spirit of true identity in Christ. If someone is fearful, pray a spirit of peace over her.

As uncomfortable as it can be to pray for your friends, imagine my surprise when I felt prompted to pray a blessing over my dishwasher repairman. He and I chatted while he worked on the dishwasher. He shared some of the hard parts of his story. How he had been physically ill and couldn't work for years. His challenging family life and losing his kids in a custody battle. After he finished fixing the dishwasher, before heading out the front door, I asked him if I could pray for him. And even more awkwardly, if I could put a hand on his shoulder.

Then, instead of starting to speak, I stopped and silently asked God what He wanted to say to encourage this man. And I listened. As words came to my mind, I began to pray them out loud. When I finished, I opened my eyes to see this grown man wiping away tears.

That's God's power at work through me to those around me. Not because I have some unique gift, but because I considered asking God before I rushed in with what I thought was needed.

I've done more damage to relationships when, in pride, I attempted to solve problems. And I've been overwhelmed when I think it's up to me to fix a friend's situation. But there has been grace and freedom when I stop and ask God first.

May we humbly ask and accept help. Intentionally seek out safe people to vulnerably share feelings. Extend invitations to walk alongside someone just a step ahead. And provide the kind of community that gives space to process, heal, and bless others.

Isolating Idea
I have to figure out motherhood on my own.

Connecting Truth
I deepen relationships when I allow others to help me.

Discussion Questions

1. Have you ever gotten to the end of yourself? Have you had a panic attack or suffered from anxiety? What has helped you? Did you go see a counselor?

2. Who are the safe people in your community? How can you help foster safe conversations with your friends?

3. What area of your life would you like to develop? Can you think of someone in your community who is a step ahead of you in that area? If not, take a moment to pray and ask God to open your eyes to a possible mentor. If so, think about when you will ask her to meet with you one time.

4. Have you ever prayed a blessing prayer for someone? Would you consider trying to pray over a friend the next time she shares a challenge with you?

Six

Cleaning Muddy Purses

Isolation in motherhood is when no one seems to understand you or reach out to you. Especially when my views and philosophies differ from the majority of the people around me due to my conservative nature. You feel downtrodden and alone. No friends, no accountability, no fellowship.

—Shannon

Being homeschooled from third through eighth grade, I don't have many traditional elementary school memories. I do remember inviting Jesus to be my Savior during kindergarten nap time. And I can't forget my lovely second-grade teacher, Mrs. Pope. She had kind eyes and a constant smile. She encouraged me to be who God made me to be and accepted me just as I was. Which I needed, because even though I'd professed faith when I was in kindergarten, the sanctification process hadn't really kicked in yet. So I was basically a real jerk in the first grade.

Most books on friendship comment on how easy it is for kids to connect with one another. Marveling at how kids can become fast friends in mere minutes. While that may be true, there were some of us kiddos who were not so accepting. My childhood friends tend to remind me of how cliquey I was. Definitely could have been cast in a prequel movie, *Mean Girls: The Early Years*. But one memory stands out as particularly horrible.

To delay sharing that embarrassing moment, let me set the stage with a lesson on '80s trends. A decade that stands out in iconic fashion—from neon leotards, parachute pants, and one-handed glitter gloves to permed hair in scrunchies. Most of us can imagine what to wear to an '80s-theme party.

But have you ever considered bringing a Bermuda bag? A less often celebrated trend of the time. This cloth (often reversible) purse was uber popular during my elementary school years. If you're curious, please google "Bermuda bags" and note the delicate pearl buttons connecting the cloth to the wooden handle—the ultimate preppy accessory.

One gal in my clique not only lived in a mansion but proudly owned a Bermuda bag. Not just any version but a white eyelet embroidery one, the envy of every little girl on the playground. Perhaps to rub it in a little more, our group decided to take turns holding the purse in one hand while going down the big slide (you know the one visible across the entire playground).

All was going well until we decided to be "nice." A girl outside of our club asked if she could take a turn holding the purse and going down the slide. We looked at the purse owner and she shrugged "sure."

That's when it happened.

She misjudged the speed of the big slide. Catapulting off the end, she not only made a hard landing on her buttocks, but the Bermuda purse flew out of her hand and into a mud puddle. We could have responded with, "Are you okay?" or "Don't worry about the purse we can clean it." We could have.

Unfortunately, our response was a bit less gracious.

"What have you done? I knew we shouldn't have trusted you! You better get that purse totally clean or you're going to have to buy her a new one."

Then it went from awful to worse.

While she scrubbed the purse clean in the bathroom sink, we stood nearby whispering to one another, mocking her mistake. Of course, the cruelty became too much. Tears fell as she dropped the purse and ran out of the bathroom. We soon found out she reported the story to our teacher, who then gave us an appropriately delivered lecture on treating people with kindness and love.

The fact that this situation stands out in my memory proves the effectiveness of her lecture. Life itself would provide its own lesson. A few years later I got a taste of my own medicine as the left-out homeschooler, and I gained sympathy for the new girl and outsider.

Honestly, I'd rather share my friendship mistakes as a seven-year-old than reveal the many I've made as an adult. We expect children to be childish, but we expect adults to know better. Unfortunately, the cruelty displayed in my story creeps into our mom friendships. Perhaps one reason we often "mom alone" is to avoid the pain of being the one rejected and hurt . . . again.

My friend Kris Habashy used to tell me, "The enemy isn't creative. He's crafty." I believe some of his go-to tactics start with the letter *d*: distraction, discouragement, and *division*. If we don't address the hurt and make things right, the enemy wins. He divides women who need one another in the mission of motherhood. Truthfully, it takes more than just one good friend. Like the adage goes, we need a village.

I hope you know that by writing this chapter I'm not claiming to have friendship figured out. In fact, maintaining friendships is a challenge for me. But through interviewing other women and making plenty of mistakes, I've gathered some "Gal Pal Guidelines." Helpful tips to keep a relationship connected and healthy even through differences and conflict. Because it's rare to leave this world without a few (or several) friendship wounds. In fact, when I asked my email subscribers to share stories of past mom conflicts and reconciliation, their stories broke my heart. Unnecessary pain caused through the very relationships God gives us to grow us.

Unity Doesn't Mean Uniformity

Let's start by addressing my first-grade clique. A clique is defined as "a small group of people, with shared interests or other features in common." Now I don't think it's wrong to have close friends. It's natural for us to be drawn to those with similar values and interests. Jesus taught the crowds and had twelve disciples, but He spent a lot of time with three men: Peter, James, and John. What differentiates Jesus's three from a clique is the remainder of the definition, "and does not readily allow others to join them." Jesus was far from exclusive. He was also perfect, so there's that.

Let's dig a little deeper into what makes cliques so appealing. For starters, in each of us there is a desire to be a part of a team and a cause. To belong. When it comes to mom friendships, my personal insecurity is compounded by insecurities about motherhood. Wanting to be a good mom so badly, my parenting ideals pull me into relationships with women who agree with my "right" way. And I tend to reject relationships with moms whose differing opinions make me feel "wrong."

I remember hosting my first baby playgroup. Sitting on the couch, I listened to a mom expound on why she didn't give her son a pacifier (while mine happily sucked away on his). Then another mom shared all the evils of letting a baby cry it out. I silently replayed the night before with multiple failed attempts of letting our son cry himself to sleep. With each expressed differing opinion, I felt less sure of my parenting choices and less connected to the women around me.

94

Fast-forward and similar conversations could be heard from the sidelines of a soccer game. The actual (and metaphorical) team lines drawn between public school moms, private school moms, and homeschooling moms. You can see moms chatting with their posse. But even at the most conservative, Christian, classical private school, you will find parents with different views. Like moms who don't see eye-to-eye on how to handle technology, for example.

If I'm not careful, I can begin to judge other moms and create a new version of my first-grade clique. Being in community with like-minded parents feels safe and seems to help me follow the formula that I've decided develops perfect adults. But does it? Am I missing out when I narrow my friend group to women who look/think/act just like me?

Thankfully, because we've been at the same church for more than sixteen years, I have friends from different school systems and areas of town. Unfortunately, because of the way Dallas was zoned (aka Jim Crow laws) there is not a lot of ethnic or racial diversity in my friend groups. It requires intentional effort to make friends outside of my school and church communities. Cultivating those friendships goes beyond proximity (being in each other's presence). I have to make time to listen. To hear another perspective. Instead of just trying to convince a mom that my way is best based on *my* experience, I can stop and listen to her story, history, and experience. And get curious.

God does not call you and me to be the same. In fact, Paul highlights the beauty of diversity in his letters. Each member of the body doing its different thing. "If the whole body were an eye, where would the sense of hearing be? If the whole body were an ear, where would the sense of smell be? . . . As it is, there are many parts, but one body. . . . But God has put the body together, giving greater honor to the parts that lacked it, so that there should be *no division in the body*" (1 Cor. 12:17, 20, 24–25, emphasis added).

Thankfully, there is no other mom who thinks exactly like you. Unfortunately, this means at some point you will disagree with other moms. The key is navigating how to maintain unity in the midst of difference. My first tip comes from C. S. Lewis, who said, "Our divisions should never be discussed except in the presence of those who have already come to believe that there is one God and that Jesus Christ is His only Son."[1] While Lewis was referring to matters of theological differences staying among believers, I want to lean in to the phrase "except in the presence of." So often conflicts are worked out virtually through social media or text conversations instead of in person.

Using digital means to sort out a conflict leads to misunderstandings and hurt feelings. I need to see your eyeballs. I need to be able to touch your hand. I need you to sense my warmth and love for you if we are going to have a conversation.

"Conversation" is the key. Have a conversation, not a monologue or debate. There is a significant difference between debate, discussion, and dialogue. "Dialogue is collaborative; two or more sides work together toward common understanding. In dialogue, one listens to the other side in order to understand and find meaning and points of connection. Dialogue involves a real concern for the other person and seeks to not alienate. Dialogue creates an openness to learning from mistakes and biases. In dialogue, finding common ground is the goal."[2]

Instead of trying to convince a mom that homemade baby food is the best option for my child's nutritional health (a stance I held only with my oldest child and quickly dropped after having multiple children), I approach the conversation with curiosity: "That's a different view from my own. Help me understand your perspective." How would our mom friendships be impacted if instead of criticism of her way, we engaged the conversation with curiosity?

Say It to Her Face

My tongue has gotten me in plenty of trouble. When I am in a bad place emotionally, I center conversations around *other*

96

people instead of myself. Whether you call it gossip or not, talking about others when they're not around has hurt many of my relationships. I can't remember the exact situation that finally convicted me. But I decided to challenge myself to only talk about someone if they were with me. I called it the "say it to her face" challenge.

As with breaking any bad habit, I needed supernatural help. My first step was to pray each morning, "Lord, put a guard over my mouth and watch over the door of my lips [Ps. 141:3]. Do not allow any unwholesome talk to come out of my mouth but only what is helpful for building others up, according to their needs [Eph. 4:29]. Amen." I also prayed this before meeting with a friend, attending a social event, or spending time with extended family.

Because I knew reshaping this habit would be hard, I created a framework for what "say it to her face" meant:

1. When in a conversation, don't talk about ANYONE unless she is physically present.
   • Even if she is a common friend (if we both know her, it's still not okay to talk about her).
   • Even if I am speaking well of her (it's a slippery slope!).
   • Even if I am just stating facts.
2. Keep her confidence. If someone shares information with me, it is not my job to share it with other people.
   • Even if it's exciting news (pregnancy, marriage, job). Remember, that's her news to tell.
   • Even if she needs prayer. Only share if she told me to ask people to pray for her.
   • Even if someone asks me a question about a person not present. I will gently direct them to that person ("You should ask her").

3. Instead of talking about others, ask the person I'm with these questions:

- What is God teaching you lately?
- What was your highlight/lowlight this week?
- What specifically can I pray for you?

Perhaps this challenge seems a bit strict or legalistic. I'm definitely not offering it as prescriptive to being a good friend. I'm also not suggesting I do this all the time. This was a personal conviction that I had to break a habit (a conviction I'm feeling again as I reread my own book!). It also helps me be a safe friend so others can be more vulnerable with me, like we talked about in the last chapter.

Like Dr. Alan Loy McGinnis says, "Nothing causes people to clam up and to abandon friendship more quickly than to discover that you have revealed a private matter. If you are a leaky repository, others are sure to learn of it. When you tell one other person a fact told to you in secret, you identify yourself to the listener as an untrustworthy confidant. Someone does not have to be very smart to conclude that if you would tell someone *else's* secret, you'll probably tell someone else *her* secret."[3]

Believe the Best

She greeted me with, "Did you get my text?"

In the hustle of getting four boys out the door, I hadn't seen her text. And it bothered her. She wondered if I was bringing my boys to an event. If so, it would help her convince her son to come. When I didn't respond, it made her night a bit trickier.

Thankfully, we easily worked it out. She apologized for leading with such a strong accusation and admitted that since her son struggled with social anxiety, in truth, knowing whether my kids were coming wouldn't change his hesitations. Lastly, she let me know she's working on communicating less combatively and asked if I would forgive her. (Of course I did! I'll need her to return the forgiveness favor soon enough.)

These misunderstandings are going to happen. But assumptions complicate things. Especially if I examine someone's actions with my motivations. What if beyond just wanting to know if we were coming, she thought I was purposefully avoiding her texts? Or because of her son's social anxiety she feared that my kids weren't coming because they didn't like her son? None of these thoughts would help resolve the misunderstanding, but only disrupt the relationship further.

When I find myself in a conflict with a friend (or having yucky feelings), I consciously stop and ask myself, "Am I assuming the best or the worst of my friend?" More often than not, if I approach her actions with love, the offense goes away. Let's work through some possible scenarios. Here are some false narratives I've thought based on a friend's actions:

- She didn't call me back because she's mad at me.
- She never goes to lunch with me because she doesn't like me.
- She didn't make the effort to say "hi" to me at the party because I'm not important to her.

Here's the reality:

- She didn't call me back because her life is as full as mine.
- She went to lunch with someone else because that person invited her. Doesn't mean she wouldn't also go to lunch with me if I reached out.
- She never made her way over to say "hi" at the party because she had to leave early to pick up her son from a football game.

99

In her book *The Friendships of Women*, author Dee Brestin uses an analogy of "roses and alligators." She said women are like roses, beautiful, unique, dazzling, but "lurking beneath the glossy, green leaves of roses are surprisingly nasty thorns." Dee goes on to say, "When a rose gardener is jabbed by a thorn, she realizes the rose had no personal animosity toward her but was simply born with thorns."[4]

Sometimes we treat our friends like alligators. As soon as we experience something hurtful, we run away instead of covering offenses or confronting lovingly. I've been guilty of treating a prick from a thorn on a rose as if it's a bite from an alligator. If you are pricked by a thorn, instead of running from the friendship (or canceling the friend), you can choose to confront in love and forgive.

Confrontation is never easy. That's why I prefer the term I learned in college: "CARE-frontation." The slight change reminds me of the heart position going into the conversation—out of care, not to get even. Before I barge into a conversation with how offended I was by someone else's actions, I need to stop, calm down, and examine my part. Author Lynn Hoffman offers four questions we can ask ourselves:

1. What happened?
2. What do I think about this situation and person?
3. What did I want (expect)?
4. How do I feel (now and any related past feelings)?[5]

Lynn also encourages you to consider if you have unrealistic expectations of other people. Are you trying to force them to be someone they are not or do something they are incapable of doing?

When you decide to care-front, not with your previous childish approach but a more mature approach, start by offering forgiveness to yourself and the other person.

I sometimes use the words "This is how I've been experiencing you lately" and share the perception of our relationship. Then I ask, "How have you been experiencing me?" Often, when I ask that question, I learn how I've unintentionally offended my friend. Once we've both shared, I offer amends for my part of the conflict without expecting an apology from her. Then I prompt a discussion about what we each would like the relationship to be in the future, sharing expectations and desires.

Even if you walk through these steps and offer thoughtful carefrontation, your words may be received as an attack. The listener can reject you and shut you out. The only way forward is to walk out that forgiveness with unconditional love and be set free.

Whenever I think of forgiveness, I think of an image Lisa-Jo Baker shared with me. It's one Paul uses in the book of Romans when he says, "Who will rescue me from this body of death?" (Rom. 7:24). The "body of death" comes from Roman culture. "Romans came up with the most unique ways of executing people (evidenced through the crucifixion of our Savior). What they would do if a murder occurred was take the corpse of the murdered person and strap it to the back of the one who committed the murder. They were required to live with the rotting corpse on their back until they got infected by it and they died."[6]

The enemy would love to hold you back in developing new friendships by strapping on every failed, dead, past relationship to your back. Letting the rotting corpse eat you from the inside out. Jesus offers a way out: drop the bitterness of the past and move forward through the miracle of forgiveness.

Set Healthy Boundaries and Expectations

Friendships have a natural ebb and flow of extreme closeness and drifting apart, and both come with a degree of discomfort. If you're too close, you may need space. If you're apart too long, then you miss each other. But, as one author points out, "If we interpret the natural drifting apart as betrayal, then out of hurt or anger we may become the betrayer."[7]

The area I've found tricky to navigate in mom friendships is mismatched expectations. Some moms are good at staying in touch with regular text messages, phone calls, and visits. Other moms are fine if you see one another every once in a while. The frequency doesn't impact how they feel about you or your friendship.

I've had friends confront me because they felt hurt by my lack of initiation in the relationship. I hadn't invited them over or asked to meet for coffee. Or called them to see how they are doing. My response is to apologize and to let them know I don't even talk to my mom very often. I also explain that I have limited time and my first priority is my husband and my kids. It's not a personal rejection of them but a protection of my time and resources.

John Townsend advises,

> If you go to Proverbs 4:23, for example, Solomon says, "Guard your heart for from it flow the wellsprings of life." And what he's saying there is that you've got to take care of your energy and your heart, your emotions. You've got to take care of yourself. You've got to have time for you. If you don't guard that heart, then the wellsprings of life won't come out from it. And when you think about the dilemma of a mother who was a life-support system for kids, if she's not guarding her heart and saying no when she needs to say no and not being as available as she needs to be for other people, she won't have the wellsprings of life for her children. So, boundaries are basically about how to set healthy, loving limits in our life. So we have something to offer to our children.[8]

Typically, if someone asks me to meet at a park or go out as couples to dinner, I'm all in! But rarely am I the one who extends the invitation. Should I initiate more? Probably. But does it mean I care less about my friends? Absolutely not. The key is to set and communicate appropriate expectations for friendships I want to maintain.

If a friend doesn't understand how I am wired and continues to expect more than is reasonable for me to provide in a friendship, then boundary lines may need to be drawn. But it's hard to draw those lines because we could hurt someone. Here are some of Dr. Townsend's thoughts on the difference between hurting and harming:

> We're supposed to be disrupting each other at different times. And if all we have is people that do nothing but say positive stuff to us and we say positive stuff to them, and we never tell them the truth, we're going to get sick. And they're going to get sick. But hurt is very different than harm. When we harm someone, we damage them. We make them lose faith or it causes bad things to happen to them. So when you say, "How do I set limits in a way that people will love it?" I haven't found that out. When my wife and my friends set limits with me, it hurts my feelings. I go, "Well, that was a bummer. So I talked too much of the party last night." But it helped me. It didn't harm me.[9]

If my feelings are hurt by boundaries others have placed on me, I need to consider my expectations and the health of the friendship. Licensed professional counselor Shundria Riddick offers these questions to consider in evaluating the health of a friendship:

- Were you able to set boundaries in that relationship?
- How do you benefit from that relationship?
- Does that relationship have reciprocity?
- Do you feel supported or isolated in that relationship?
- Does your friend offer space for you to be yourself?[10]

Shundria says, "We usually test the health of a relationship because sometimes relationships end. That's okay. People can go their separate ways. It's fine." But it hurts. We can acknowledge that pain and heal, not letting the "break up" define us or our ability to be a good friend.

Of course, you and I desire the perfect friend. Solomon wrote, "What a person desires is unfailing love" (Prov. 19:22). The Hebrew word for "unfailing love" is *hesed*. We want people in our life to provide mercy, kindness, *and* faithfulness. We need people to be both kind and loyal. But they will fall short. Here's the good news: "Jesus is never tired of me always needing Him. Instead, He is delighted by how desperately I need His validation and He never, ever withholds it from me. Or from you."[11]

The key is to realize God is the only true source of *hesed*—unfailing love. "When a friend lets us down, we show our theology is off-base when we're overcome with shock. When people let us down it confirms what Scripture says, we are all sinners and none are righteous."[12] But when we let God be the center of our lives, He becomes our base of security and source of *hesed*. We realize "God's love isn't based on me. It's simply placed on me. And it's the place from which I should live: loved."[13]

Here's the good news: you and I are invited into the best clique—in communion with the Father, Son, and Holy Spirit. From that place of full acceptance and unfailing love, may we offer curiosity in our differences, thoughtfulness in our care-frontations, forgiveness in our misunderstandings, and gentleness in setting healthy boundaries.

Isolating Idea
I avoid conflict if I disconnect from others.

Connecting Truth
I can disagree with you and stay united.

Discussion Questions

1. Friendships are not easy. If you are willing, share with the group a time you caused another friend pain and your friendship ended.

2. Consider your current friendships. Are there a variety of gifts, perspectives, and interests represented? What could you do to expand the diversity in your friend group?

3. How would you feel if your friends took the "say it to her face" challenge? How would it change how vulnerable you are with them?

4. Share about a time when your actions were misinterpreted by someone or you misinterpreted someone else's actions. How did you resolve the misunderstanding?

5. What boundaries have you found helpful in friendships? How have you been hurt by someone else's boundaries?

seven

All Working Moms

"Do you think this is a sign that you should stay home with your kids?" A well-intentioned woman asked me this question after I'd finished an extremely hard week managing my full-time job and four young children. I'll never forget the way it made me feel. Maybe I misunderstood what God was asking me to do. I stayed at home for seven months with my first child before making the decision to pursue my career. I thought staying at home was "the right thing to do," but during that short season, I felt an overwhelming call to pursue work outside the home. I'd be lying if I said I haven't second-guessed this decision many times. Being a full-time working mom of four is isolating in its own way. I'm misunderstood often.

—Lindsay

How does the saying go? "The best laid plans of mice and men often go awry"? In early 2020 I told a group of author friends my detailed plan to finish writing this book before my boys got out of school for the summer. Unfortunately, with only half the book written, the world shut down as the COVID-19 virus spread across the globe. All four of my boys were sent home to finish the school year. A bit ironic to be writing a book on fighting isolation while sheltering in place. In an unprecedented moment, millions of people found themselves experiencing the grief, frustration, and loneliness many new moms experience. It can take a mom years to acknowledge the isolation of mothering. To grieve the loss of her life before kids. To find purpose in this new assignment. And now a huge number of people processed the transition to life at home while physically distanced from others.

During the pandemic, online experts, communicators, and celebrities offered encouragement and perspective. Including these words from the Today Parents Instagram account written by a contributing psychologist, Emily W. King:

> Parents: What we are being asked to do is not humanly possible. There is a reason we are either a working parent, a stay-at-home parent, or a part-time working parent. Working, parenting and teaching are three different jobs that cannot be done at the same time. It's not hard because you are doing it wrong. It's hard because it's too much. Do the best you can. When you have to pick, because at some point you will, choose connection. Pick playing a game over arguing about an assignment. Pick teaching your child to do laundry rather than feeling frustrated that they aren't helping. Pick laughing, and snuggling, and reminding them that they are safe. If you are stressed, lower your expectations where you can and virtually reach out for social connection. We are in this together to stay well. That means mentally well, too.[1]

Dr. King is highlighting our physical and emotional limits as human beings. But what was interesting is how moms rejected her encouragement. One mom wrote: "I've worked from home and homeschooled for 11 years. It's not impossible but it's also not for everyone." She makes a good point. There was a year where God directed me to continue to produce the podcast and homeschool two of my boys. It was the fall after my dad passed away. My mom was living with us and receiving cancer treatment. I was working, parenting, teaching, and "daughtering."

While it wasn't impossible, it also wasn't easy or sustainable. In order to fill all those roles, I had to say no to other demands. "No, I can't chair Pioneer Day. I'm homeschooling, working, and caring for my mom." "No, I can't travel to speak." "No, I'm not able to write an endorsement for your new book." With a tendency to say yes to anything that helps move me forward in my social life or career, I found that having these clear boundaries helped me to better see what wasn't mine to do. It also gave my soul space to grieve and recover from the stress of earlier that year.

Back to the quote from Dr. King, another mom commented: "This seems a bit smug. Some of us (not myself thankfully) do not have employers who understand that you still have to care for a child, or two or three, while you still work and perform at 100 percent. Please reconsider assuming that everyone has the same privilege as you do. Because many moms do not, and they see this as a luxury issue. Many moms are debating much, much worse, like which kid gets food and which one doesn't."

I agree that being able to choose working outside the home or staying at home is a privilege. Lowering work expectations is a privilege. Being able to feed all your children without fear of how to pay for it is a privilege. But I think Dr. King's focus wasn't on those factors but on how we can choose to connect instead of perform. How do we lower the pressure to be all the things to all the people? And no matter your socioeconomic status or position, that's an internal posture. When I stood chatting with the migrant teen mom in Mexico, she chose connection over performance. Her child sweetly fell asleep in her arms while we talked. In another migrant center I met a teen mom who gently cared for her infant who had a cold. Her entire focus was on survival. She and her sister and their girls had fled Guatemala because her brother-in-law had tried to kill her sister. When I arrived at the center, these sisters were packing up their things. They'd reached their limit of stay (fourteen days). They had no money and nowhere to stay. While her six-month-old slept on the bottom mattress of a bunk bed, through a translator we heard about their plans to sleep on a bench in a park that night. They also told us about an aunt who was a bus ride away in Mexico. All they needed was money for the bus tickets.

These moms weren't debating whether they should stay home or work outside the home. They were wondering, *Do we sleep on a park bench tonight or figure out a way to make enough money to get to our aunt's house?* Thankfully, our team secretly gave them a small amount of cash to help deliver these girls safely to their family and security.

So, what does this have to do with the debate over staying at home, working from home, or working outside the home? My hope is that instead of arguing about which choice is "right," we will choose connection—within our family and to other moms.

During the pandemic I was on a video conference call with Dr. Henry Cloud. He was helping us understand the neurological and psychological response to the crisis. Interestingly, he compared our bodies to a house and said that how we "stand" in the midst of shaking reveals our physiological integrity or the wholeness of our mental/psychological structure. The foundation to our house/selves is a sense of "bondedness" or connectedness to God and people.

He referred to babies adopted from orphanages where their physical needs were met but they lacked emotional connection with another human. He also shared how a brain MRI reveals black holes resulting from that kind of neglect. Our brains were literally wired for connection.

When we find ourselves stretched or shaken by changing circumstances, like transitioning to being a stay-at-home mom or going back to work, he suggested checking in on your connection points. Consider your relationships like a series of concentric circles. He

110

referred to Jesus, who was intimately connected to the Trinity—the innermost circle. Then the next ring was His relationships with His close friends, Peter, James, and John. He then engaged with all of the twelve disciples—the next ring. And the outer circle was the community or masses around Him.

How would you map out your relationships? Who would be in your circles? And no matter what job you hold, in what parts of your day/week/month are you intentional about staying connected to those people? I'd advise that those in the tighter rings would get the majority of your time and attention. Those in the broader circles are relationships that you maintain but aren't prioritizing over the inner circles.

A Mom AND . . .

After trying to encourage a mom with the formula, Average Mom + Perfect and Loving God = Best Mom Ever, she asked, "If that's true, me + God = Best Mom Ever, does it matter that I stay home? I have a good friend who didn't choose home but stayed in the workforce and has two kids. She seems really happy, and her kids appear to be doing well. Do you think I should go back to working outside the home?"

(*Side note: I know I'm entering dangerous territory. For clarity purposes, this discussion will not include the issue of financial need but will focus on a mom's heart.*)

Personally, I always wanted to be a stay-at-home mom. Dreamed about it. Carefully nurtured my six different Cabbage Patch Kids. And yet I also wanted to go to medical school and become a pediatrician. In college I worked hard for good grades, took the MCAT, even applied to medical school. But once I had an engagement ring on my finger and plans to move to Chicago, my doctor dreams were replaced with a new pursuit—video production (I even sent résumés to Veggie Tales and Oprah's production company . . . and, no, I didn't get either job).

Then I worked as an elementary school teacher's aide. During that time, I discovered speech-language pathology. When we moved to San Francisco, I volunteered at a hospital helping kids with auditory processing disorders. Then back to Chicago to get a master's degree. Then we moved to Dallas, where I helped rehabilitate children with cochlear implants.

I switched things up a lot.

Once I had my first baby and stayed home for hours a day, I was bored.

Don't get me wrong. Being a mom was the *hardest* job I'd ever had, but it just wasn't meeting a couple of my deep needs. One need I have is for outside approval, and the other is a need to accomplish tasks. Staying home I found there were no A+'s or teacher accolades or peer congratulations. I never finished a task without it needing to be done again several times that day. In my situation, as a stay-at-home mom, I needed an "AND." An extra something. A place to get that approval and accomplishment.

So I became a stay-at-home mom AND a college professor, teaching one class a week.

Then a stay-at-home mom AND a part-time speech-language pathologist.

Then a stay-at-home mom AND a MOPS registration coordinator.

Then a stay-at-home mom AND a blog writer and podcast host.

The "AND" was usually shoved in the margins—during afternoon nap time or while kids were in school or late at night or early in the morning. I sacrificed other things, like a favorite TV show or lounging on the couch, to make space to do the "AND" things.

Back to my friend I mentioned above who asked, "Does it matter if I stay home? Couldn't I work outside the home and still be a great mom?" Ultimately this question needs to be answered by her and God. Because every woman's story is different.

For me, being maternally driven, I *wanted* to stay home with my kids. It was not because I think it's the "right" choice, but because it's what I wanted, and given our economic position, I was able to. I have many friends (and family) who have managed full-time, outside-the-home careers and made fantastic memories with their kids in the margins. Unfortunately, due to my poor time-management skills, I would miss out on cracking open pecans we picked from the backyard. Or snuggling up on the couch reading lots of books. Or enjoying our version of teatime.

But I have needs, like approval and achievement, that my children cannot fulfill on a daily basis. So that's where my "AND" place comes in. Finding something to put focus on and gain immediate satisfaction from so I can be a satisfied woman. Then from that place of fulfillment I can pour more love into the lives of my children.

Of course, there is a delicate balance. Only you can know your motives. Ask yourself, "Am I escaping motherhood with my 'AND'? Or is it adding to my experience as a mom?" Sometimes we think it's all or nothing: full-time job on Wall Street OR stay-at-home mom. The most important thing is to seek God first. He will show us if the "AND" is adding or detracting from the life He desires us to live. When I am reading the Bible daily and praying, the Holy Spirit gives me a nudge when I am off track or right in His will.

For me, having an "AND" models for my boys how they can use the gifts and talents God has given them for His glory. I remember my mom going to speak at women's retreats or leading discipleship groups at our kitchen table or taking college courses. She often had an "AND." I knew she was seeking God's plan. She was fulfilling her calling to "make disciples" and listening to God on where her next assignment was to fulfill that calling. Like the game-changing distinction one of my guests, Kat Armstrong, shared, "If you follow Jesus then you've been given the same calling, 'To go and make disciples.' And throughout your lifetime you've been given various assignments to live out that calling."[2]

There is freedom in each of us following God and His unique assignments. How He has wired and placed me is going to be distinct from you. So instead of judging someone's "AND" choice, we can connect and cheer them on.

Your Mom Brand

Remember the teen moms I met in Mexico? I confidently labeled them "good moms." Their lives looked nothing like the "good mom" formula we hold in our minds. Thankfully, there are more than just two kinds of moms. There are thousands of different brands of moms. The world and your kids miss out when we believe anything else. Based on my story and other moms I know, it's likely you will rebrand a few times based on circumstances and family needs.

In order to come alongside each other in mom friendships and to thrive in whatever work environment we find ourselves, it helps to identify our unique mom brands. Then you and I won't feel the need to defend or excuse who we are but can embrace our brand and encourage the mom next to us to do the same.

How do you find your mom brand? Here are some questions to ask yourself:

What do I value?

Values direct decisions. If you value cleanliness, then you will prioritize spending time and energy keeping a clean home, car, and life. If you value creativity, you are likely more comfortable with a bit of chaos in your home and unstructured spaces to create. A person who values faith will make the time to connect with God and a faith community. As a mom, what do you find matters most to you? Kendra Adachi encourages us to "embrace what matters, ditch what doesn't."[3] This is not based on what Pinterest tells you "should" matter most. But what kind of life brings you the most joy? When you imagine a good day, what does it include?

What are my current assignments?

Often, moms struggle to embrace motherhood because it doesn't feel like a satisfactory "calling." Or they thought it would be more fulfilling than it is. That is why Kat Armstrong's distinction between calling and assignments (that I mentioned earlier) is helpful.

114

As a follower of Jesus, you have your calling: to go and make disciples. Now some questions to consider are, What assignments has God given you? Where has God placed you to make disciples? Who is He asking you to live in proximity with and model faith to in everyday interactions? Where can you use the gifts, talents, and interests He has given you?

What assignments am I struggling to accept?

Motherhood is one of the assignments to live out our disciple-making calling. What are some of the *other* assignments you've been given? What circumstances are part of your story today? The answers to those questions impact your brand of mothering. If you have an ill parent who requires your attention, then you're not signing up to bring cupcakes to the class party. If you have been assigned to reconcile your marriage impacted by infidelity, you may not have the time or energy to join that girls' night out.

When we're given harder assignments for a season, we need to give ourselves grace when our mom brand looks different from others. And we acknowledge that rebranding may be around the corner. These assignments are not always permanent.

How does our family flourish?

One day I opened a letter from Samaritan's Purse. In it was a picture of a mom and her four boys seeking shelter in a cave because of the war in South Sudan. Her family's flourishing did not include a trip to Disney World or even a nice dinner out. Flourishing for them meant fleeing violence and finding security. So often "flourishing" is overcomplicated with comparison to the top 1 percent of wealth in the world. Instead of looking around at what other families are doing, consider what helps *your* family flourish.

In order to be approved by others, my friend Aubrie decided to leave a job she loved and stay home full-time. Over the next several months I watched the light and joy leave her countenance. Wearing sweatpants, hair in a ponytail, and making minimal eye contact, it was obvious to anyone she was far from flourishing. Fast-forward a few years, after doing some inner work and processing in community, she (and her family) is thriving. She works on staff for our church, has been promoted, is smiling and filled with purpose. Her kids are happy, her marriage is improved, and their family unit is connected and content.[4]

I'm sure Aubrie isn't the only one who has tried to fit someone else's mold for her. In fact, author Jo Saxton said, "It took me awhile to get comfortable in my own skin. And to realize my stay-at-home friends weren't judging me. The ones who judged me, I didn't become friends with. My friends wouldn't judge me anyway. They saw themselves as part of my support network."[5] The better we each identify our brands, the better support network we become. I hope you take the time to answer those questions to figure out your values, your assignments, your challenges, and what helps you flourish. If you're like me, perhaps it would help to read about a few different mom brands.

Let's start with my friend Charity. She values international travel and experiences. As a part of that, she and her husband adopted two boys from Ethiopia. Her current assignments include moving away from a successful business she started to a new city to have more time with her family. While she struggled to find contentment in her new space, they flourished by continuing to travel internationally as a family. And they recently felt led to move back to her hometown for more support from friends and family.

Another friend, Jeni, values homeschooling her four kids. Tragically, because of her husband's abuse (and for the safety of herself and her children), she was given the assignment of single parenting. Thankfully she has the skills to help online entrepreneurs grow their businesses. In her brand of mothering, she has been able to work from home and teach her children so that her family can flourish.[6]

I could chronicle a thousand different brands of moms. And there is no ranking order of one over another. I see them each as valuable. The less we judge one another, the better we can support each other.

Isolating Idea
I don't belong because of my career choices.

Connecting Truth
I have a unique mom brand and you do too.

Discussion Questions

1. Have you struggled with the decision to stay home, work outside the home, or work from home? What aspects of that decision are challenging (identity, family finances, child's well-being)?

2. Take a moment to draw a relationship map based on who you'd like to have as your priorities. Who do you have in the various levels of your concentric circles? Now consider your daily time allotment. Who gets a majority of your time? What do you need to change in order to be intentional and stay connected to the people who matter most?

3. Write up your brand of mothering. What do you value? What are your current assignments? What assignments are you struggling to accept? Where is your family flourishing?

4. Is there a mom you may have been judging for either staying home or working outside the home? What's one way you could support her this week?

eight

Keep the Candles Lit

I wanted to be a stay-at-home mom and feel so blessed that I am able to be. And yet I miss achieving outside the home. I resent my husband who gets a break, can use his brain in a different way than I do, accomplishes tasks, and gets compliments for his work and raises from his boss. I was tired, didn't always like being a mom, and wanted to run away a lot. I thought I was the only one and I was doing something wrong.

—Jessica

"Make sure you twist your feet to crack your ankles before he falls asleep. Pat his back softly, then slow to a stop. Keep your hand on his back for a little while. Then once you're sure he's asleep, crawl out of the room through the bathroom sliding door, which makes less noise."

Dear friends and babysitters, I'm sorry we were bossy first-time parents and gave such ridiculously detailed instructions for putting our firstborn to bed. It wasn't you, it wasn't even really "us," it was me. And you weren't the only ones I micromanaged.

Enter Bruce, my husband.

On paper, Bruce and I grew up in very similar homes—each set of parents married for almost fifty years, his dad a doctor, my dad a lawyer, four kids in each family, raised with Christian values. But once a little person entered our home, we quickly saw how differently we approached parenting. Both wanting to do a "good job" but approaching the task with our own definitions of "good."

Let me give you an example.

One evening Bruce came home from work. As a loving, involved dad, within seconds of getting home he asked to hold the baby. Because my husband likes to play and laugh, he wanted to play and laugh with our son. In the words of *The LEGO Movie*, "Commence micromanagement . . ."

"Don't toss him in the air. I just gave him his medicine and fed him. If he spits up, I'll have to give him more medicine."

You see, our oldest son had severe reflux and any little jostle led to a vomiting mess. Not only did I want to avoid a mess, I felt pressure to help this baby grow. And if he spit up a lot, that's milk that isn't digested. If he didn't get enough milk, he wouldn't grow. I worried I'd look like a bad mom who didn't take care of her son's basic needs. In Bruce's mind a good dad holds, plays with, and engages with his son. That includes tossing him in the air. In my mind a good mom gives her son enough milk so he can grow.

Can y'all relate? Have you and your spouse had differing views on what is "good" for your child(ren)?

On that particular day an additional layer of insight popped into my head. I told Bruce that since I had left my full-time job to stay home with our son, I saw this job as important. Reading books from experts, getting advice from the doctor, and chatting with friends, all with the goal of doing the best job I could do.

When Bruce came home, he jumped in to do the same job I'd been doing all day. If he didn't see my "instructions" as valuable, it felt like he viewed the job as if "anyone can do this." And it made the role feel less important. I asked him, "What if I walked into your office, sat at your desk, and started messing with one of your spreadsheets, but you weren't allowed to say anything about what I should do? Wouldn't you feel a bit anxious?" He countered back with understanding but also a desire to connect with our son and contribute to the family. He felt belittled and controlled while trying to be a dad.

So we came up with a solution.

We decided to give Bruce ownership of certain aspects of our son's routine. Having Bruce oversee bedtime felt like a good place to start. That way he could deal with any issues that came from *how* he chose to put our son to bed. And I could take a break from the job I'd been doing all day.

Let's take a moment to acknowledge the gift of having a husband who wants to bond with his son and help me care for him! Y'all, I almost strangled that desire out of my spouse with my need to be a "good mom."

Thankfully, fifteen years later, Bruce still does the bedtime routine. There are so many sweet memories made during bath times, reading books aloud, and laughter. All because we communicated about our differences and connected on a solution. I share our story not to make you feel bad if your hubby doesn't help with bedtime but to consider your own differences and encourage you to communicate on how to work together.

You Complete Me

I posted a poll on Instagram asking how moms differed from their spouses in parenting. Some responded there wasn't enough space to list all the ways. Another simply typed "omg." A lot of gals easily found differences. Maybe you can relate to their list:

- He is quicker to correct.
- I'm strict, and he is easygoing.
- He is a helicopter parent, and I let them live.
- He is more of a yeller, and I speak softly and slowly.
- He gives in, and I die on every hill.
- We agree on the rules, but he doesn't enforce them.
- He is more gospel-focused, and I can't let go of legalism.
- He is cautious, and I'm a risk-taker.
- I'm more emotionally connected, and he's less emotional.

Doesn't it make sense that two different humans who grew up in different homes and have different personalities would approach a task as monumental as parenting differently? And yet in the moment-to-moment home stress we forget. We expect the other spouse to respond and react just like we do. But how boring a world it would be if all humans were created the same.

I also asked the gals, "When have you found the different way to be better?" It seemed several of them had an aha moment when considering a response. They went from freaking out about a spouse's faults to being thankful for balance. They said they found a spouse's approach better when

- his attentiveness prevents accidents;
- the kids try to get away with something;
- he prioritizes relationship over rules;
- he gives grace more;
- the oldest child enters the teen years and needs guidance.

One mom communicated it best when she said, "Life goes better when I put more faith in him as a person instead of in my own will and desires." Faith in him as a person. A person with his own unique perspective, personality, and experiences. A person who can join you in this parenting journey instead of being shut out or undervalued.

When Bruce and I were doing premarriage counseling, the pastor asked us how we wanted to handle lighting the unity candle. Confused, we asked what he meant. He went on to explain that some couples use the individual candles to light the larger unity candle and then blow out the candle they each hold. Other couples light the unity candle and keep the candle in their hand lit.

In that moment we naively (and wisely) declared we'd keep our individual candles lit. The word *synergy* had been a big part of our dating relationship. We talked about how bringing two people together was more powerful than just 1 + 1. Marriage to us was more of an exponential equation. The combined energy being more than just the sum of its individual parts, with a potential for even greater productive power.

So, yes, light the unity candle to symbolize two becoming one. But keep our personhood candles lit because our unity benefits from our individual flames—in work, in friendships, in faith, and in growing the kind of family we desire.

In order to keep a flame lit, you need to make time to figure out how each partner is wired. How do they see the world? What gifts do they bring to your parental leadership? This may look like taking a StrengthsFinder test or studying the Enneagram.

"With the Enneagram, you can see that we all struggle," says gospel-based Enneagram coach Beth McCord. "We all need Jesus. It's just we need Him in different ways. And He makes us more like Him in different ways as well. It's called the body of Christ, and we reflect Christ differently. We all need to bring our uniqueness to glorify Him and bless each other."[1]

For years whenever Bruce reloaded the dishes in the dishwasher after I'd filled it, I thought it was a critique on my dish-loading skills. Then he took the StrengthsFinder test and we saw one of his top strengths is "maximizer." His behavior was reloading the dishwasher, but the why behind his action was trying to maximize how many dishes were washed.

Once I recognized his strength, I interpreted his actions differently. Less about my discomfort and confusion and more about his motivation. Like understanding why he had to do "one more thing" before we head out the door when we were already late going somewhere. He was maximizing. Or changing plans at the last minute . . . maximizing.

Instead of seeing what he was doing with the same reason why I would be doing it, I saw with new eyes. And our marriage communication improved. Instead of being hurt, confused, and frustrated, I simply told myself, "Oh, he's maximizing right now." My heart filled with more grace and love than criticism and judgment.

Discovering our individual strengths also meant exploring our weaknesses. In doing so we discovered neither Bruce nor I have the strength of deliberativeness, which is taking time to consider a decision and all the options and potential outcomes of your choice. Knowing this led us to intentionally take more time than is natural for either of us to make decisions and hopefully to prevent future resentment because we made a bad choice.

Beth McCord shared how acknowledging different perspectives helped her marriage.

> So, my husband is a type six on the Enneagram, the loyal guardian, and I'm a type nine, the peaceful mediator. So, it's like he's wearing orange glasses and I'm wearing purple glasses. And when we look at the same circumstance and he doesn't do what I think he should do or say what I think he should say, I can get very irritated because I think everyone sees the world through purple lenses. And I'll think, "Why did you just do that? You must have meant to hurt me or you must have meant to do this." And that's when we assume incorrectly other people's thoughts, motives, and behaviors. Because we think theirs should be like ours. That's what we call "assumicide," where we incorrectly

assume other people's motives and we get frustrated. We end up hurting, and eventually, we can destroy our relationship when we incorrectly assume.[2]

Another helpful tool Bruce and I use to avoid "assumicide" came from a Brené Brown Netflix special.[3] It's a simple concept with tremendous ability to repair relationships. If you find yourself in a conflict with your spouse, simply use the phrase "The story I'm telling myself . . ." to share your perspective on the situation.

For example, "The story I'm telling myself when you reload the dishes is that I shouldn't even bother doing the dishes because you think I'm a dishwasher idiot." In return Bruce might say, "The story I'm telling myself when I reload the dishwasher is that by rearranging, we could fit a few more dishes and maximize this washing cycle." Boom. I had interpreted his actions as personal, and he was simply trying to save our family money.

Connection Points

For centuries moms have debated which transition is harder—zero to one kid or one to two kids (all the parents of multiples are shouting, "I'll tell you what's hard!"). Here's the deal. With every addition to a family, there is an opportunity for transformation. Our regularly scheduled mode of operating no longer functions. We can't fall back on yesterday's systems to manage today's chaos.

Honestly, we often don't give the transitions enough credit. Yes, they have the potential to derail family structure. But with a bit of creativity these "comfort disrupters" can lead to deeper family connections.

You've already read about how Bruce and I devised a plan to help with my micromanagement issues in parenting our first child. When boy number two came along, we slipped into a pattern of me caring for the newborn while Bruce took on responsibility of our oldest son. Granted, when I was home full-time, I managed both boys. But typically, when our family was together that's how we split up our roles. Bruce with the big kid(s) while I handled the new baby.

Unfortunately, that "divide and conquer" approach didn't give either of us time to rest and recharge. Once the boys were asleep, instead of hanging out together, we'd find separate spots in the house and veg out on our computers (today's version would be smartphone scrolling). About seven months into kid number two, we had a "come to Jesus" moment. The lack of kid-free time together meant a lack of between-the-sheets time (wink, wink, you know what I mean).

It made sense. Having a newborn or infant is physically exhausting. Multiple young kids hanging off my body made me super disinterested in additional physical touch. Not to mention the impact of hormone changes. Throw in how disconnected I felt emotionally. Often, the last thing I was thinking about was making love. But then there was the nagging thought, "I *should* have sex with my husband if I'm going to be a good wife."

I love my husband. But I often felt like loving him "that way" was more of a duty than a delight. Until my friend Francie Winslow gently reminded me how important having sex was to our connection, our family, and even our community. "Sex is a multiplying factor in our lives, not just with producing kids, but producing a massive amount of connection. God is an invisible God who wants to make himself visible to us. When man and woman come together as one, it's his invitation for humanity to become one with God. Intimately connected with Him."[4]

Believe me, I understand bringing up this topic unleashes a thousand other topics and wounds, defensiveness, and hurt. Even *that* fact reveals how important physical connection is—the vulnerability of intimate moments. How physical intimacy leads to emotional intimacy, like a circle of arrows, one feeding the other, and when one stalls, the other does as well.

You know what's easier in the short run? Isolating. Focusing on your own needs and waiting for your spouse to make a move to connect. Making that first move toward your spouse is sacrifice. Once again, God never asks us to do anything He wasn't willing to do first. He left heaven and embodied an infant (the fullness of vulnerability) and sacrificed His body so we could experience eternal intimacy with the Father.

God invites us to fight for connection instead of fighting one another. To choose unity over the natural bent to singularity. All while the enemy throws his favorite strategies at your family structure—divisiveness, distraction, and discouragement. When we push past our desire for comfort and extend ourselves physically to a spouse, we claim victory. Our legacy gets a bit stronger. A society benefits from our stronger union.

Honestly, my interest in being intimate is directly correlated to how emotionally connected I feel to Bruce. Like those arrows I mentioned earlier, married life is good when those arrows move between us in a positive direction. Having regular *connection points* helps cover up for any misses in our parenting correctness.

Before having kids, our standing "date" was Saturday brunch. Bruce traveled a lot for work, but we knew he'd be in town on Saturday mornings. We'd often do a two-thirds, one-third split of whatever savory option he ordered and sweet breakfast I ordered.

But this connection point became trickier with toddlers and newborns to entertain while chatting. So, after our "come to Jesus" moment in 2010, we implemented "meet me on the couch" (zero points for creative naming). Basically, after putting the toddler and newborn to bed, we'd meet on the couch. And not to watch TV. We would swap stories from the day or just sit together for a bit. It was a way to remember we liked each other.

Another way we remembered liking each other was taking twenty-four-hour staycations. Basically, either my parents or a babysitter would come over for Friday night and stay until after naps on Saturday. We'd enjoy a nice dinner out and an evening at a hotel (Priceline can have great last-minute rates), and we'd sleep in, read books, and enjoy Saturday brunch. Incredibly life-giving to our marriage.

I can't remember when we started one of my favorite connection points. But it is simple, free, and impactful. Each morning before we take the boys to school, while they finish breakfast and gather up backpacks, Bruce and I meet in the kitchen, stand in an embrace, and take turns praying for each other. These aren't long, eloquent prayers. But typically we hear what's on the other's heart and mind. What's causing stress. What's coming up that day. What's going well. And it only takes five minutes or less to show our boys that our marital connection and dependence on God comes before anything else that day.

The connection strategy with the biggest impact on our marital communication came from a conversation with Shauna Niequist.[5] She told me about her friend in New York City who would bring the baby monitor and chat with her husband on the fire escape. Based on their tradition, Shauna and her husband would say "fire escape" and meet on the back patio.

I heard her idea around the time my parents moved in with us. Meeting on the couch was no longer a good option for chatting. So our "fire escape" became morning walks around the neighborhood. Bruce was between jobs at the time, so we took almost daily morning walks while my mom stayed home with the boys. Eventually we moved the walks to Saturday mornings (our original marriage connection time of the week). And now with older boys, we leave one cell phone at home with them, take a phone with us, and stay within a block's distance. Shoulder-to-shoulder chats are a nonthreatening way to share our hearts and career hopes and to realign parenting strategies.

Lastly, there is incredible power in shared experiences. Sometimes these are planned. Like the time Bruce's coworker invited us on a free trip to Cabo, Mexico. We arranged for my parents to stay in Dallas with our boys. Despite the trip starting off with my lost luggage, we made great memories. We tried deep-sea fishing for the first time (and discovered we both get really seasick). The highlight was when Bruce and I swam with dolphins. Dolphins, y'all! A once-in-a-lifetime shared experience.

Sometimes, magical moments just happen.

We'll never forget the time good friends asked us if we would go out to dinner. They were struggling in their marriage and asked if we could go to a quieter restaurant to talk. Now I can't remember if I'd told Bruce that last part before he made the reservation. But he decided to look for a new restaurant with great reviews, which led him to El Ranchito.

With crowds of people waiting outside and music blaring, before taking a step inside I worried this wouldn't quite offer the quiet ambiance we needed. As the hostess sat us front and center, I noticed not only large parties celebrating but also that we were the only non-Hispanic patrons. Kudos to Bruce for discovering a legit (and amazing) Mexican food experience, but it held more of a fiesta than siesta vibe.

As I took in the surroundings, our friends arrived. We exchanged looks acknowledging this wasn't exactly what they had in mind. But to leave at this point would be incredibly rude, so we started munching on chips and salsa. Our friends began to share a bit of their marital challenges. Bruce and I leaned in, not only out of concern but to hear the words coming out of their mouths.

That's when it happened.

We heard them before we saw them. Not one, but two mariachi bands started playing at full volume. In that moment our friends stopped talking and we burst with laughter. Just as we caught our breath from laughing so hard, we looked up to see disco balls twirling above our heads and multicolored lights flashing. Complete and utter chaos. And it was fantastic.

When we calmed down from laughing at the lights, I looked up to see one of the mariachi bands had made its way over to our table. A trumpet's horn blared six inches from my friend's husband's head. We again lost it, filled with indescribable joy.

129

By the time we'd paid our check, contagious happiness replaced any stress our friends had previously felt. And our El Ranchito shared experience went down in history as the best way to heal marriages.

It proved true once again recently. Unbeknownst to us, the couple we'd invited to join us at El Ranchito had a huge fight that morning. Only two minutes into our dinner, they shared with us that they were not in a good place. Once again, the mariachis and life-giving ambiance (and some good group processing) led to a better-connected couple by the end of the evening. And lots of laughs.

Don't get me wrong. I'm not suggesting that if you are struggling in your marriage all you need are chips, salsa, and a good mariachi band. I am saying that there is power in doing life alongside other couples and in sharing the hard parts and laughing together. And some professional marriage counseling with that goes a long way.

Staying connected to your spouse is hard work. But the intentionality of choosing each other, even in your differences and because of them, makes your family stronger. Because one day (hopefully) your children will grow up and move out, and it will be just the two of you once again. My mentor, Leslie, has married off three of her four boys, and all four boys have left the house. The first year as empty nesters, she and her husband intentionally set aside time in their calendars to reconnect without kids. She told me how much easier it was to reconnect because of all the time they had invested in being together while her kids still lived at home. And how seeing their parents prioritize marriage has set her boys up for success in their own marriages.

Prioritizing reconnection is important because the odds are stacked up against our marriages. Like Paul David Tripp says, "What's a biblical view of marriage? Well, it's a sinner married to a sinner in a fallen world. Are you encouraged yet? But with a faithful God. Now that means we can't just coast in our marriage because there are things inside of me and things inside of my wife that are potentially destructive to marriage because we're not perfect people yet. And we live in a fallen world that is a threat to our marriage."[6]

A sinner married to a sinner. This means abuse can enter into your relationship. Or adultery can break your marriage commitment. Or addiction can disrupt trust. My hope is that if you find yourself in a similar place, you can reach out to someone who has been there. You can get the professional help you need. You can ask God to give you community support. I can't imagine a more important time to not mom alone. Most importantly, I pray, if possible, for marriages to be reconciled. If not, for God to work in the individuals' lives to heal wounds and bring personal life restoration.

Beth Moore shared such a miracle in her marriage. She longed for her husband to be the spiritual leader, and she held a "Cinderella marriage" expectation. When her reality fell short, she shifted that expectation to her relationship with Jesus. "Don't misunderstand me, that did not drop Keith down. It just put things in their proper place. It meant that I didn't expect of Keith what only Jesus was going to be able to deliver to me."[7]

May you and I hold in proper place the role of a spouse in parenting. May we work *with* one another to be the best well-rounded parenting team possible. To intentionally pursue connection points. And to allow Christ to do His work in delivering us from ourselves.

Isolating Idea
I need a more helpful parenting partner.

Connecting Truth
I value connecting to a parent who is different from me.

Discussion Questions

1. How have you and your spouse approached parenting differently?

2. What do you appreciate about how your spouse does things differently from you?

3. Have you studied StrengthsFinders or Enneagram? If so, share with the group how the results of those tests helped improve your marriage.

4. I shared ways Bruce and I connect emotionally to help connect physically. What are some ways you and your spouse stay emotionally connected throughout the week? Any funny shared experiences?

5. Take a moment to share current marital challenges (without blaming your spouse or giving advice) and pray for one another.

Connected to Your Child

nine

Don't Make Me Angry

Without question, the times I've condemned myself the most and felt the worst are the days I've yelled at my kids and lost control of my anger. The reason is that yelling is the one thing I remember telling myself I would never do as a Mom. Not only did I mistreat my kids with my words, but I stepped into a family pattern I promised myself would end with me.

—Tracy

The time had come.

A moment I'd carefully planned with a sliver of hope for success. While my children and husband complained about inconvenience and uncomfortable clothes and being forced to stand in formation and smile on command.

Yes, the dreaded Christmas card picture day had arrived.

Perhaps like me you wonder, "Why do we still send out Christmas cards?" Not only are they expensive, but they seem a bit unnecessary with social media keeping us up to date on how tall Johnny is this year. The torture of capturing the perfect picture should be reason enough to drop the tradition. Plus, there's the pressure to make sure the clothes are color coordinated, but not too matchy-matchy (at least we have Pinterest to consult). And, of course, the entire family must look happy and connected. All for the purpose of sending out a filtered version of the true narrative in celebration of Jesus's birth.

I don't mean to go all Scrooge. But there have been years we should have skipped the Christmas card pictures in order to prevent relationship damage with my boys. It's hard enough to keep clothes on four boys or keep them seated during dinner. Apparently, my concern for your approval outweighs my desire for peace in our family. I kid, I kid. Sorta.

One photo session stands out in my memory. We arrived at the city park right at dusk, as instructed. The boys (aged two to eight) spilled out of the car. Thankfully the photographer (a high-energy guy himself) immediately began taking pictures. The boys had made a beeline to climb a short wall and then miraculously stood in a line facing the photographer.

All was going well until the middle boys started spinning into their silly modes. Behind the photographer's back, I gave them the "I'm serious" face. Then mouthed harshly, "Stop it!" with accompanying mimed instructions to Calm. Down. Right. Now.

My intention was to prevent the synergy effect of high-energy boys. You know the synergy effect? How if one boy goes off the rails, we lose the whole crew to pure chaos. And we hadn't even taken the coveted family picture yet!

Even though I hadn't yelled or thrown things, my just-below-the-surface anger had made its impact. If I could show you the resulting pictures, you'd see back-to-back photos of my middle boys full of joy then squashed down to forced smiles. And all these years later I find it a bit humorous how dramatically their expressions changed from one moment to the next.

Which picture do you think I'd want hanging on my wall? The one showing the fullness of their personalities? Or the one with crushed, unnatural expressions?

Yeah, you guessed right.

Of course, I chose a pretty benign anger story to start off this chapter. There are plenty of moments in my mothering journey when I've yelled so hard and often I've lost my voice. I've slammed countless doors in anger. Said words I wish I could take back. And cried buckets of guilty tears over a day "ruined" by my anger. I never in a million years thought I would be an angry mom. In fact, since yelling was a part of my upbringing, I'd created an informal vow with myself never to yell at my kids.

In talking to lots of women over the years, I know this topic is a tender one. There are childhood wounds that lay festering under the surface. A loved one's expressed anger caused lasting pain. So I don't enter this conversation lightly. Please know that you are not alone if you've experienced abuse of any kind. There are professionals willing and able to walk with you toward healing.

I also know that there are millions of moms going to bed with the guilt of wondering if their anger injured their children that day. The same moms who cut sandwiches into butterfly shapes and sing lullabies over their children at night. Women who desire so greatly to be a "good mom" and feel completely defeated when anger surfaces.

Here is my tricky question: Is anger actually bad?

The answer is a bit complex and makes me think of the Hulk (stick with me).

One day my boys stumped me by asking if Hulk was a good guy or a bad guy. I'm definitely not a Marvel expert. I did know Hulk was a part of the Avengers, and they were good guys. Then again, he did so much damage as a ripped, green, impulsive giant. Was he good or bad?

Do you remember the classic Hulk line?

137

Dr. Bruce Banner would warn, "Don't make me angry!" He knew anger unlocked the destructive Mr. Hyde nature of the Hulk. If he could stay calm, everyone else would be safe.

So, is that the key? Never get angry?

I don't believe so.

For centuries, Bible scholars have considered the texts on anger and asked the question, "Is anger a sin?" In the late thirteenth century, Thomas Aquinas addressed the topic in his work *Summa Theologica*. Scriptures like Psalm 4:4 and Ephesians 4:26 instruct us to be angry *but* not to sin. Aquinas noted, "The movement of anger is not in our power."[1]

We will get angry. The emotion will move through us. Because God made us in His image. Over and over again He reveals His anger toward the Israelites who turn away from Him. Jesus in the temple was angry with those who were profiting financially inside His Father's house. We know God is holy, and Jesus is without sin. If They both experience the emotion of anger, then feeling angry is not bad.

From a cursory review of Scripture related to anger, I noticed a pattern. God warns about being quick to respond in anger (Eccles. 7:9; Prov. 14:29). He advises against befriending those who are hot-tempered or easily angered (Prov. 15:18; 22:24). And He warns not to give full vent to anger (Prov. 14:29). Which reinforces that the key is less about not getting angry and more about *how* we get angry. Instead of giving in to the energy of anger and fully expressing it, the key is to recognize it and respond with self-control.

The first step to dealing with anger in motherhood is taking note of your emotions. Naming them instead of reacting from them. Of course, this is hard to do in the moment. So often, as a weary, busy mom, if someone asked me how I was feeling, my response would be, "Tired." Unfortunately, being tired is not an emotional state but a physical one.

Through our church's recovery program, I learned to pay attention to what I was feeling. While there are differing opinions on how many emotions we experience, most trauma and recovery programs focus on eight primary emotions: pain, anger, joy, passion, guilt, shame, fear, and love. I found it helpful to practice labeling emotions with a safe group of friends. Once a week, we gather with our small group and share our dominant emotions and process them together.

If you've been given the message from those around you that feelings are not important, remember we are made in God's image with feelings. If we don't acknowledge them, name them, and choose how we will respond to them, then we find ourselves in trouble. Think back to the garden of Eden, when Adam was told by God to name the animals. In doing so, Adam was given dominion over them. In a similar way, when you label your feelings, they don't get to boss you around. You are less likely to react from them and harm the people you love most.

Once you get better at identifying your feelings, the next step is to investigate the cause. Ask yourself questions like, *Why is my stomach tight? What am I scared of? What am I sad about? What is overwhelming me right now? What am I thinking? And is it true?*

I wasn't always an angry person. In fact, if I could pick a dominant emotion from my childhood (and even into adulthood), it would be fear associated with a lie of weakness. In believing a lie that I was vulnerable and weak, I had many fears. I acted on those fears by hiding. At bedtime I would lie still, with my covers over my head, convinced a thief would look in through the window. If he saw me there, he would attack me. But if he couldn't see me, he'd move along.

As a mom, anger started to grow as my fears and vulnerabilities grew. The more boys I had, the more independence they gained, the angrier I became. I've come to learn that the anger was secondary. Psychologists Jeremy Safran and Leslie Greenberg say,

> Some clients express anger when experiencing an underlying feeling of vulnerability. We hypothesize that in this situation the feeling of

anger helps to maintain a sense of self-esteem. . . . The therapeutic task here consists of accessing the underlying primary emotion. . . . For example, the client who experiences feelings of vulnerability may be able to learn to ask for support rather than distancing people with anger.[2]

Which circles back to the first few chapters of this book. Trying to mother on my own instead of asking for help from others led to an increase in angry outbursts.

The key is to do the investigative work outside of an intense moment. Become an objective observer, taking note of patterns in your emotions, thoughts, and actions so you can break the cycle of anger. Your "why" is going to be different than my "why." And the solution for you will be different than mine. When we get to the root cause, we can lose the guilt associated with anger and respond more to the real problem instead of just trying to stop yelling.

This truth came from my aha moment while reading *Good and Angry* by Scott Turansky and JoAnn Miller. They say, "Anger is good for identifying problems but not for solving them."[3] Those words helped me drop the guilt and refocus my energy. Instead of just trying *not* to get angry, I wanted to figure out the cause of my anger.

Figuring out the cause during a heated moment is a bad idea. For most of us, there are only milliseconds between a trigger (whether internal or external) and an angry reaction. Trying to think objectively about anger while angry doesn't make any sense. Thankfully, experts and authors have done the work for us by writing chapters on various triggers with guidance on how to train character instead of disrupt connection. My friends Amber Lia and Wendy Speake wrote a book called *Triggers: Trading Angry Reactions for Biblical Responses*. When Amber came on the podcast, she wisely said, "There is nothing anger can do that love can't do better."[4]

Like a Badger

Tracking my triggers helped me realize why I kept getting angry with one of my boys in particular. Maybe you can relate to the situation.

While I cooked dinner, my four-year-old came in the kitchen and asked if he could have a cookie. I calmly responded with "No, I'm making dinner. If you eat a cookie now, you won't be hungry for the food I'm cooking. Maybe we can have a cookie after dinner."

Just a few minutes later, in walked the same child: "Mom, can I have a cookie?" A bit confused but still composed, I said, "No, sweetie, you can't have a cookie. I'm making dinner."

Then again, "But I want a cookie. Can I have a cookie?"

Cue angry reaction.

"No! I've already told you no. Stop asking me! You cannot have a cookie!"

Thankfully, Turansky and Miller dedicated an entire chapter to this exact situation. With their help I was able to realize why his repeated requests weren't just annoying but made me angry.

He was badgering.

Yes, that's also the name of an animal. You may have seen that episode of *Wild Kratts* with the video of a real badger digging a hole with his nasty long claws.

In fact, once I realized the source of my anger, I used that children's TV show clip to communicate and teach my son about badgering. I borrowed the script from Turansky and Miller, saying, "When you ask me the same question over and over, it's called 'badgering' and it hurts our relationship." Even at four years old, he understood what I meant. At one point in my lesson I may have even demonstrated persistent digging with my fingers, which became our very effective sign for "You're badgering!"

From that point on, when he would ask me the same question repeatedly, I would start to get angry. But instead of yelling, "Stop! I already answered you!" I simply used our digging sign. The anger helped me identify the problem, and now I had another way to solve the problem, which in this case was a character flaw. Turansky and Miller point out, "Sometimes the badgering is simply an attempt to gain attention and lots of it. . . . Children who use badgering tend to be self-focused and can't see what their barrage of questions and comments is doing to relationships. . . . Badgering is a selfish way for children to get what they want."[5]

Just like any character flaw, there's a hidden strength that needs refining. By recognizing what was going on in my son's heart, we could address the issue to decrease the tension and distance in our relationship. "Instead of getting into the boxing ring with your child, imagine going around the ring to the child's corner and becoming a coach."[6]

Honestly, that annoying persistence has been shaped into a helpful asset. This son works diligently on his middle school homework without any nagging reminders—a skill that makes parenting easier in the preteen years. One that wouldn't have been refined if I'd continued to simply respond to his badgering with anger.

It's helpful to analyze the times you get angry. What are your triggers? What's happening? Who is involved?

I'll go first. My anger is triggered by

- sibling rivalry,
- being late,
- a cluttered house,
- a strong-willed child,
- homework battles, and
- disobedience.

For several of those triggers, I've examined what needs to be trained in my child, what expectations of mine need to be adjusted, and what is going on in my heart.

142

I Can Only Control Myself

"What if the key to changing your son's behavior is to change your behavior?" Frequent podcast guest and calm-parenting expert Kirk Martin's words burned a little bit going down. He followed it up with another hard truth: "Heather, you can only control one person. Yourself."[7]

Ouch.

I'd been trying to control others using anger. Yelling "Stop it!" at a mid-tantrum toddler only worked half the time. And when it *did* work, the child was more terrified of me than connected to me. Remember when I mentioned earlier how fear and weakness led me to resort to an energizing emotion like anger to help me feel more in control? Dealing with my fears of failure, rejection, and pain helped loosen the grip of anger.

Honestly, Kirk's advice that I could only control myself sounded like a lot of work. Reining in my thoughts, emotions, and actions could be a full-time job. Kirk coached me to chill out, pointing out how invested I was in wanting my kids to behave, which led to me whining and handing over control.

So, Kirk encouraged me to be "an impartial giver of wisdom." To offer advice about how to behave in an even, matter-of-fact tone. He said that acknowledging their frustration ("I can tell you are really frustrated") could calm them *and* me down. If I tried that approach, I wouldn't be ignoring what's happening but addressing it with a leadership tone.

He suggested that if a child is upset, parents should model a calm response. One way to do that is through movement. He said, "Motion changes emotion." You can't "think" your way out of being upset. The middle of a tantrum is a terrible time for a lecture. Instead, after acknowledging the child's emotion, a parent could sit down and start coloring or build with LEGOs. This sends a message to the child that you are in control, so they can be in control. Invite them into your calm space. Kirk encouraged

143

parents to choose a neutral body posture like sitting or lying down, because it's hard to argue from those positions. Picture a dad and his teen son lying on the ground having a calm conversation versus standing face-to-face yelling at one another.

One of my favorite ideas Kirk shared was for the dad shopping in Walmart when the kids are wiggly and driving him crazy. Instead of getting angry at them and losing it in the frozen food section, Kirk suggested dropping to the floor and doing push-ups. That change in position would calm the dad down (and build muscle mass . . . win, win). The kids would be so confused about what dad's doing that they may start giggling and stop being annoying.

Another thing Kirk got all up in my business about was self-care. He said, "If you don't care enough to take care of yourself, physically, emotionally, spiritually, why would anyone else care?" Once again, he was right.

Some days I just need to drink a glass of water.

For reals.

Have you tried it? If you're finding yourself irritated repeatedly, go get a glass of water. Finish drinking it before you do any more analyzing of why you're angry. Like I said in chapter 3, you are a physical, limited being who needs water to survive. When your body doesn't get what it needs, it goes into survival mode, which usually isn't your happiest place.

Perhaps in the constant pouring out, we forget the beautiful complexity of how God made us: a spirit-filled soul with a body. Each of those parts—spirit, soul, and body—require care. They each give us signals that something is wrong, but in our busyness those signals get ignored.

Let's talk about a simple example. When you step on a LEGO, the skin on the bottom of your foot gets stretched. Under the skin, nerves are alerted and they send a message to your brain. Your brain then sends a message back down to your muscles to pull your foot up. Most likely you will scream out or mumble

144

frustrated words of how these kids never pick up their toys. The neural messages sent to your brain protected you from further harm. I mean, who wants a LEGO permanently embedded in the bottom of their foot. Not I!

I don't have to explain to you how a mom's day is filled with physical activities (especially during the little years). On top of being physically drained, her sleep is interrupted, so she can't even recover. Fueling her body with the nutrients she needs is often not at the top of her mind. So, of course, when children misbehave, a worn-out mom is going to react with anger.

In this case, the anger may be secondary to pain. The body is crying out for rest. Perhaps the anger is really guilt from wanting rest but putting her kids' needs before her own. In taking care of her physical body, she is able to better care for the needs of her kids.

Remember how I said a human is a spirit-filled soul with a body? It's helpful to imagine our composition using concentric circles. The outermost circle being the body and the innermost circle being the spirit (and for the believer in Jesus, that is where the Holy Spirit dwells). Then picture the space between those two circles as representing the soul. Although there has been a lot of debate over how to define the "soul," the definition that aligns best with Scripture includes will, thoughts, and emotions.

When the soul goes unchecked, it gets pulled between your body's natural response and an unnatural, godly response. For example, in exhaustion my body (or "flesh") pulls strongest on my soul. That's when I want things my way. My thoughts are lies, and my emotions (anger, fear, shame) are directed toward getting control. But when I'm leaning into the Holy Spirit (that center circle), I'm surrendered to God's will for my day, my thoughts are more aligned with truth, and my emotions look more like the fruit of the Spirit ("love, joy, peace, forbearance, kindness, goodness, faithfulness, gentleness, and self-control" Gal. 5:22–23).

I shared how my anger acted as a warning signal of a deeper issue of fear. Recognizing what triggered my angry reactions caused me to dig deeper into the why behind my anger. Why did I need to control others? Why did I so intensely need the boys to behave? Why did I desperately need the approval of others?

Thankfully, through prayer with friends, God revealed the hold fear had on me. Yes, my soul was "saved" and God's Spirit dwelt in me, but my will, emotions, and thoughts (aka my soul) could still be broken and in need of healing. Until I presented those broken places to my ultimate Healer, they would continue to cry out in pain. Jesus showed up and removed the lies of being unsafe. He called me "beautiful" and "worthy," which loosened the grip of fear of rejection. Because what can man's (or mom's) rejection do to me if I am loved and approved by the God of the universe?

> Out of my distress I called on the LORD;
>   the LORD answered me and set me free.
> The LORD is on my side; I will not fear.
>   What can man do to me? . . .
> I was pushed hard, so that I was falling,
>   but the LORD helped me.
> The LORD is my strength and my song.
>   (Ps. 118:5–6, 13–14 ESV)

Do you see how anger can be a good thing? What a gift to acknowledge frustration as a warning sign and then with intention allow God to work. Give Him access to your kids and your soul. Let Him bring about the redemption we all long to see.

Isolating Idea

I can't stop yelling at my kids.

Connecting Truth

I can identify anger triggers and use calming tools.

Discussion Questions

1. What is a predominant emotion in your day?
2. Do you express anger by stuffing it inside or by exploding?
3. What are some of your internal and external anger triggers?
4. Have you ever taken time to consider what part of your story could be contributing to your issues with anger?
5. Whom could you ask to keep you accountable in dealing with your past and making a commitment to yell less in the future?

Like Riding a Horse

When my oldest son was two, I went to visit my sister, and my mom came with me. I was struggling with my son and had started counting to three. My mom asked about counting and I brushed her off, saying, "It just works for us!" Well, maybe five minutes later, my son ran outside and headed for a busy California road. I yelled, "Jack, stop! Jack! One, two, three, stop!" And in that moment, I realized that maybe I could at least listen to what she had to say regarding counting. Do I have the humility to listen to unsolicited advice from someone older and wiser? Or do I need to have it "all figured out"?

—Alicia

Early one morning at family camp, after pulling on too-tight jeans and too-large estate-sale cowboy boots, I opened our cabin door to find two college gals ready to watch our boys for a couple hours. We heard this was one of the best parts of family camp. An adults-only morning spent horseback riding followed by a delicious cowboy breakfast (we're talking maple syrup–soaked bacon, y'all).

I expected to enjoy doing something in nature and anti-urban. I got excited about the extra time with just Bruce and our friends. I didn't expect to be given the most memorable parenting wisdom for the week.

After a brief lesson from the head wrangler, he assigned us each to a horse. We were given the simple instruction to keep our horse facing a rope hanging down from the side of the barn. We were also instructed on the importance of these first few minutes establishing a relationship with our horse. How gently we sat down on the horse and how we took control determined how the rest of the ride would go.

I was swinging my leg around the saddle to sit atop my horse, Patriot, when my neighbor's horse, Red Baron, decided he wanted to get away from the (apparently evil) horse on the other side, Tank. Unfortunately, that meant Red Baron no longer wanted to face his rope. Instead, he wanted to turn around and head out of the barn. The shocked rider attempted to pull the rein back toward the assigned spot, but her horse was determined otherwise.

The wrangler arrived and gave gentle instruction and encouragement. "You aren't doing anything wrong. Your horse doesn't like getting close to Tank and wants to get away. You just need to confidently lead him back to his spot." Which she successfully did. But that lasted about a minute before Red Baron tried to turn around again. His rider, with fear in her eyes, was saying, "I'm not sure about this. I don't know . . ."

Maybe she was remembering our earlier lesson about the importance of establishing control. Maybe she wondered, is it okay that her horse had just broken ranks? What about on the trail ride, would he continue to go off course? Maybe she should switch horses? The wrangler arrived again with his encouragement. "You're not doing anything wrong. Gently guide him back to his position. You are doing exactly what you should do."

That's about the time I made the parenting connection.

You see, the week before we left for family camp was rough. The boys broke my heart with their bickering. I had poured out my concerns to a friend. It felt like I repeated the same phrases to my boys with no effect: "Love one another." "Be kind." "Use gentle words." "Treat your brother special." My friend encouraged me with the phrase, "Remember, mothering is discipleship."

She reminded me of how Sally Clarkson, through MomHeart, opened my eyes to see motherhood as ministry. From her time as a missionary with Cru (formerly Campus Crusade), she applied discipleship tools to mothering. Her husband, Clay, wrote a book called *Heartfelt Discipline*, which connects discipline with my horseback riding experience:

> Childhood is to be characterized by parents and children who are walking together on the path of life. You are a godly guide, directing your children in the way of wisdom and righteousness. You are training and instructing them about how to walk this path in order to find life as God intended it to be. You are also warning them about the dangers that would lead them away from the path and correcting them when they stray from the path. This fuller biblical picture of discipline reflects an ongoing relationship in which you are patiently and lovingly guiding your child.[1]

A process. A journey. Just as I continue to strive to live like Christ, my boys are following me on that path. "Be imitators of me, as I am of Christ" (1 Cor. 11:1 ESV).

We lined up our horses for the trail ride. Again, Red Baron decided to take a detour. Another wrangler encouraged the rider. "Remember, they can sense when you are afraid. They know when you lose your confidence. You are doing a great job. Just keep turning the reins back to the direction of the path."

This discipleship journey with my boys is so very similar. Like Solomon in Proverbs 4, instructing his son from what his father, David, had taught him:

> Listen, my son, accept what I say,
>   and the years of your life will be many.
> I instruct you in the way of wisdom
>   and lead you along straight paths.
> When you walk, your steps will not be hampered;
>   when you run, you will not stumble.
> Hold on to instruction, do not let it go;
>   guard it well, for it is your life.
> Do not set foot on the path of the wicked
>   or walk in the way of evildoers.
> Avoid it, do not travel on it;
>   turn from it and go on your way. (vv. 10–15)

My kiddos will continue to go off track. I shouldn't be surprised or fearful or personally offended. Like I said in the last chapter, responding with anger, hurt, or fear will not help get them back on the right path. As the rider gently directs the horse back in the direction it should go, I can respond firmly and gently, not emotionally or reactively.

My friend that morning feared what the rest of the trail ride would look like if she lost authority with her horse. Often, I fear what the rest of my boys' lives will look like if they act out or misbehave. I project their future selves instead of focusing in the moment on leading gently back to the path of righteousness. When the boys go off course, I simply need to steer the reins back to center.

Just like the wrangler encouraged, God gently whispers, "You are not doing anything wrong. Your son is behaving just like a little boy. He needs direction. Continue to guide him. You are doing a great job."

My listeners' number one favorite topic on the podcast is discipline. It makes sense. Like I've said many times before, you and I want to mother well. There has been a shift in how parents handle discipline since our grandparents' or even our parents' generation. Of course, every generation wants good behavior in our children, but how do we shape it? How do we handle bad behavior and make sure it disappears?

Over the years hundreds of books have been written on the topic. There is no way I could summarize all that literature in one chapter. I wish I had a nice, neat spreadsheet to give you with specific scenarios: "When your child _____, then _____." Unfortunately, my kiddos are still in process (aren't we all?), so I don't even know if any methods we used actually worked. But I have had the privilege of chatting with lots of parenting experts who have reared children into adults. I've noted their humility. They agree with my statement that we are "important but not essential."

In matters of discipline, it is important to remember you are a steward helping shape your child into whom God created them to be. You're not working to craft your child into a trophy to make you look better or investing emotional energy into chiseling away an idol who gives you value or worth. Paul David Tripp says, "If your eyes ever see or your ears ever hear the sin, weakness, and failure of your children, it's never an interruption, it's never a hassle, it's always grace. God loves that child. He's put him or her in a family of faith, and He will expose the need of that child to you so you can be a tool of His rescue and transformation. That's parenting."[2]

To go back to the horse analogy, I vividly remember attending a speech-language pathology conference. The keynote speaker that year was "The Horse Whisperer"—a man who had changed the way wild horses were handled. Instead of "breaking" a horse, he would gain respect, establish relationship, and then train the horse. Right there in the Fort Worth Convention Center we watched as he artfully interacted with a wild stallion. He was never harsh but was successful in gaining the horse's trust. We found out that this famous horse whisperer also fostered forty-seven children. His gentle and kind approach had helped these children grow into beautiful men and women. Isn't that God's way with us? "God's kindness is meant to lead you to repentance" (Rom. 2:4 ESV).

Connect, Then Correct

So many days I wish I had a discipline formula to follow instead of being led by the Spirit. In a moment of chaos, I want control. I want children to be a blessing to others. Thankfully, gospel- or grace-based discipline doesn't mean letting your kids do whatever they want.

Like Paul David Tripp offered, "Your children need law in their lives. Law does a great job in exposing sin. It's a wonderful guide for living. But what's important to understand for parents is the law has no capacity whatsoever to rescue and transform your children . . . none. If all your children needed was a neat set of rules and regulations properly enforced, Jesus would have never had to come."[3]

It's a balance of setting boundaries and embracing the gospel of Christ. Romans 8 reminds us that the law reveals sin. But it can never save us from sin. "For God has done what the law, weakened by the flesh, could not do. By sending his own Son in the likeness of sinful flesh and for sin, he condemned sin in the flesh, in order that the righteous requirement of the law might be fulfilled in us, who walk not according to the flesh but according to the Spirit" (Rom. 8:3–4 ESV).

The best biblically based framework I've encountered for how to integrate gospel relationships and rules comes from the Connected Families Ministry, founded by Jim and Lynne Jackson. They are the parents of three grown children. In their book *Discipline that Connects with Your Child's Heart*, they present a four-part framework to go beyond controlling or avoiding a child's misbehavior. The goal is for discipline to "flow from a parent's heart of humility, forgiveness, wisdom, love, and vision for a child's life. It must make sense to the child to win his or her respect."[4] Ultimately it helps parents realize that moments of discipline can be moments of connection, not frustration.

The bottom layer of the Connected Family framework (graphically represented by a pyramid) is to communicate to your child the message, "You are safe." Like I shared in the last chapter, we can prepare our hearts as parents. By analyzing our anger, we can do the work to figure out where that emotion is coming from and calmly approach our children. In fact, my hope is that this book has helped you seek God to uncover any lies you believe or hurts you need to surrender to God's care. As you allow God to work in your heart, healing past wounds and/or wrong beliefs, you will be able to communicate, "You are safe," to your child.

Personally, becoming a safe parent not only included working on my anger, but also dealing with my issues I've shared at the beginning of this book—issues of control and fears of rejection or failure. I took their misbehavior personally. A mentor instructed me to stop depending on my son's obedience for my identity. Ouch. True . . . but ouch.

Once we've prepared our hearts as parents, the next layer up in the pyramid is communicating "You are loved—no matter what." This isn't tough love or love that lets kids off the hook. "The key is to demonstrate love in ways that hold them accountable for learning, without exasperating them."[5]

Imagine a challenging scenario in your home. Is it getting ready for bed? Helping to do chores around the house? Finishing their homework without your nagging? What would it look like if instead of engaging that situation with a lecture, you led with love? If instead of yelling across the house, you got close and used a kind, loving tone.

I know this is challenging because I struggle every day to start with the message, "You are loved—no matter what." I often communicate, "You are loved if you do what I ask. But my attitude toward you turns sour if you act disobedient or disrespectful." Which is why I love Karis Kimmel Murray's "basket" method. The idea is to separate your child from the undesirable behavior and mentally place the behavior in a basket.[6] You can love the child while correcting the situation. I love you, but I don't love how you are talking to me, treating your brother, etc. This concept helped me better communicate, "You are loved—no matter what."

Really, isn't that how our Father God sees us? Because of Christ's death on the cross, He doesn't see our sin (when we miss the mark); He sees Christ's righteousness. We can be in right relationship with God because on the cross Christ dealt with our past and future sins. That doesn't give us a free pass to keep sinning. It doesn't mean there aren't consequences. But His love remains constant despite our sin. Our bad behavior doesn't disrupt how much He loves us.

Author Jeannie Cunnion helped me approach correction with humility and love when she reminded me, "Recognizing God's grace for us allows us to come alongside our kids to the cross."[7] We are all sinners in need of salvation. If I remember my own need for Jesus, I am more likely to approach my child with patience.

Sure, this all sounds lovely when you are calmly reading this book. It's another thing to put it into practice in the heat of a disciplinary moment. To help me thoughtfully respond, Karis Kimmel Murray offered some simple questions to consider: "Is this sin or simply childishness?" "Will this situation matter in ten years?"[8] Pausing to internally answer these questions, maybe you and I can approach the situation more lovingly and less reactively.

One mom emailed me after applying Karis's wise advice. This mom had been solo parenting while her husband traveled. It had been a long day. While feeding her children dinner, her son spilled his milk. And not just on the table but on an upholstered chair! Being exhausted and knowing she still had to get all the kids in bed, this weary mom said normally she would have freaked out. But thankfully she had listened to Karis's episode that day. And Karis's question, "Will this matter in ten years?" popped into her head. Realizing that in fact spilled milk on fabric is annoying but not permanent, she calmly helped her child clean up the mess. After dinner and putting the kids to bed, she went to bed guilt-free because she evaluated the severity of the situation with proper perspective.

Another favorite parenting hack for helping communicate safety and love is "Mommy Time." I learned it years ago from parenting expert Amy McCready[9] (she calls it Mind, Body, Soul Time). Basically, each child gets ten minutes of uninterrupted time with me doing whatever they choose.

While it seems silly to plan one-on-one time, in those years with lots of little ones, intentional time wasn't happening. Because of the way children are wired, without that positive attention, they use misbehavior to get attention, even if it's negative. According to Adlerian psychology, a child's primary goal is to achieve belonging and significance. Belonging is being emotionally connected, secure about his or her place in the family, and given sufficient positive attention. Significance communicates "I am capable" (which we will cover more in a minute), contributing in meaningful ways, and having personal power.

So a child is saying, "I want to belong and feel significant, but I don't know how to do it." This is when the misbehaviors, such as whining, clinging, helplessness, sibling rivalry, and tantrums, occur. If they don't get the positive attention they need, they will get it with negative attention-seeking behavior. If they don't get the personal power they need (when we order them around too much), they become more defiant.

When my boys were little, we would have Mommy Time midmorning and then again post-nap/snack before I started cooking dinner. We would draw names to determine who went first. We also set up rules that if you interrupted another brother's time, his time would start over. My goal was to be emotionally available, doing something fun of my boy's choosing (puzzles, LEGOs, coloring, chase, trains, Uno). Leading up to our time, I would say things like "Oh, I can't wait until Mommy Time," and "What are you going to choose for us to do during Mommy Time?" Afterward, I made sure to affirm our time: "I loved playing _____ with you," and "What a great Mommy Time! Thank you for spending time with me."

"Mommy Time" fits right in with the next layer in the Connected Families framework: communicating to our children, "You are capable." A great place to start is to identify the gift behind the misbehavior. For example, coaching a child who complains by acknowledging his or her ability to see problems and solve them. Or recognizing strong will as leadership/assertiveness.

Another way to communicate that your child is capable is by supporting their ability to self-correct their behavior. The best way I've found to do this is by calmly asking my boys questions. When I remember to do this, it makes the interaction less confrontational and helps my child move from defensive to analytical. But it can be hard to think of questions in the moment. Thankfully, here are a few questions from Paul David Tripp to help get to the heart level of your child's behavior:

- What's going on?
- What were you thinking and feeling as it was happening?
- What did you do in response?
- Why did you do it?
- What was the result?[10]

Let me give an example of how I might (*ideally*) use these questions. One afternoon I hear my boys in the other room screaming and crying. I first remind myself that this is an opportunity to help work on heart issues. I may ask, "Can y'all work this out, or do you need help?" If they are fighting so loudly that they don't hear my question, I calmly enter the room and ask, "What's going on?" Typically my boys talk over each other, blaming their brother for the conflict. Before I ask any more questions, I take a tip from Jim and Lynne and encourage each boy to find a space to calm down.

Once calm, we come back together and I ask one of the boys, "What was going on?" He may respond with, "He took my truck!" With a tear-stained face, the other boy may chime in, "He grabbed it back and hit me on the head with the truck!" So now I have a basic synopsis of the situation to head into the next question. I ask the boy who hit his brother on the head, "What were you feeling and thinking when you decided to hit him with the truck?" Because of our emotion chart on the fridge (hat tip to David Thomas and Sissy Goff), he hopefully responds with, "I was mad and frustrated." Then I follow up with, "What did you do because you were mad?" "I hit him with the truck." "Why did you do that?" "Because he took my toy and didn't ask me first." "What happened after you hit him?" "He cried and was sad." Then I follow the same series of questions with the other boy. Getting to the heart of what he was feeling and thinking and what he did.

When I take the time to work through those questions and coach my boys through this conflict, I teach them how to be aware of their patterns of feeling/thinking/acting. I also help attune them to the feelings of others and how their actions impact those around them. Lastly, they learn tools for repairing broken relationships, which will definitely come in handy in adult relationships.

This leads us to the top of the Connected Families framework pyramid. The last message they suggest communicating to your child is, "You are responsible." Our children will make mistakes. It isn't loving or kind to allow those mistakes to continue without natural consequences or efforts to make things right.

It is hard to give a child space to experience the impact of his or her actions. Particularly as a first-time parent with one child. Not addressing every misstep feels neglectful and unwise. When my oldest boys were young, I definitely fell into the helicopter parent category and did more damage overparenting than letting them alone.

In his book *Hints on Child Training*, H. Clay Trumbull writes, "Child training is a necessity, but there is a danger in overdoing in the line of child training. . . . Peculiarly is it the case that young parents who are exceptionally conscientious, and exceptionally desirous of duties, are liable to err in the direction of overdoing in the training of their children."[11]

Written in the late 1800s, it's just as applicable today. Trumbull goes on to quote a father who saw how his overtraining had impacted his oldest daughter. He realized it would have been better to leave her alone more. He recognized his mistake and parented his younger children with more freedom. "My rule with all my children, since my first, has been to avoid an issue with them on a question of discipline whenever I could do so safely. And the less show of training there is, in bringing up a child, the better, as I see it."[12] I agree. If I could go back to when my kids were little, I would hope to err a bit more on *under*training than overtraining.

When you put together the messages of "You are safe," "You are loved," "You are capable," and "You are responsible," a child feels supported in the training process. They believe you are on their side to see them become the best versions of themselves instead of feeling unworthy, shamed, or needing to perform for approval. Most of those messages require effort on our part to communicate. Practicing. Forgiving one another. Trying again. Just like learning to ride a horse.

Isolating Idea
I don't know how to get my kids to obey.

Connecting Truth
I can connect with my kids while shaping their behavior.

Discussion Questions

1. Share with the group how your parents handled discipline. Do you want to follow their example or try a different approach? Why?

2. Discuss Paul David Tripp's quote, "The law has no capacity to rescue or transform your child." If your role as a parent isn't to just enforce rules, how does that impact interactions with your kids?

3. Do you lean more toward overparenting or underparenting? Why do you think that is?

4. Which of the Connected Families messages is most challenging for you to communicate: "You are safe," "You are loved," "You are capable," or "You are responsible"?

eleven

Throw Away the Receipt

When my oldest was two or three years old, she was IN-
TENSE. (Now we know she has SPD and ADHD but had no
idea then.) I was friends with two other moms with girls the
same age as my daughter, and their girls were so sweet and
calm and compliant. I was so ashamed and embarrassed
by my child's behavior and they just couldn't relate to my
struggles with parenting. I gradually pulled away from
playdates and hanging out with them, and now it's been
YEARS since we've talked.

—Christin

"So when your son misbehaves at home, what kind of consequences do you give him?" The preschool teacher's question hung
in the air.

Consequences?

Oh Mylanta, in just six years of parenting I had completely
forgotten about consequences (and had yet to learn from all those

163

awesome parenting experts from the last chapter). I figured she didn't mean yelling from the other room, "Stop it!" She was probably looking for a more intentional approach, including time-outs or removal of privileges. At that stage of four boys six and under, I called it a successful day when all of my boys were fed, dressed (most of the time), loved, and kept safe. A lot of those days I spent feeding a newborn on the couch while calling out instructions for everyone to "be nice," "give that back," and "say sorry." And so, yeah, I had forgotten about consequences.

She went on to declare, "I think you're going to have a real problem on your hands if you don't get this child to respect authority." Her words felt like a future indictment.

Wasn't this the same boy whose teacher a year ago told me how sweet he was? How she loved to hold him in her lap and read a story because he was so cuddly? This same boy has an authority issue?

The hard part now of looking back on that moment is she was a bit right. Her words were the first in a long line of hard conversations with teachers. Now to be fair (if one of his teachers is reading this book), there have been several teachers who understood his challenges. They never considered him an inconvenience but creatively engaged him. More importantly, he knew they wanted his best and were for him. I guess you could say he was polarizing. Either teachers were constantly calling about misbehavior or they were singing his praises.

Maybe you have a kid like that too? The one who keeps you humble. Or maybe, like me, you have several kids helping you not get too puffed up in your parenting. Honestly, I wondered if I'd been dealt a raw deal. Wouldn't four girls be a whole lot easier? They probably don't cause as many problems in the classroom. In my mind girls sat quietly, wearing bows in their hair and coloring princess pictures. Obviously, that's a false stereotype. But it was my way to reconcile the challenge of having hard-to-handle kids. The kind of children who didn't fit the mold and who got poor reviews. Kids who made me look bad (ah, there it is).

But I *Want* It

Once again it goes back to Genesis with Adam and Eve in the garden. The enemy planted a lie, "Did God really say?" And they believed perhaps God was withholding something from them. Eve's desire for that fruit became stronger than her desire for God. That desire was wrong because God had told them not to eat it. In a moment, her coveting of something she didn't have led to disobedience and sin.

God takes this idea of coveting seriously. In fact, it's one of the big ten rules he gave Moses: "You shall not covet your neighbor's house; you shall not covet your neighbor's wife . . . or anything that is your neighbor's" (Exod. 20:17 ESV). Which includes wishing for kids like your friends' kids. Or at least wishing for a different type of kid. In the New Testament, Luke warns, "Be on guard against *all* covetousness" (Luke 12:15 ESV, emphasis added).

I know this feels like a big leap to go from negative teacher reviews to coveting. But the more I dig in my heart about what's going on, I find I'm like Eve. I've placed my trust and my hope in the idea that life would be better if I had different children.

Really the root of wishing for a different (or less difficult) child is that I'm not believing God is *for* me. Kind of like when my son's behavior improves when he believes his teacher is *for* him. When he is confident that her instruction is for his best, then he surrenders his strong will to her direction. But I struggle to surrender when I fall into the false belief of "blessings theology." The idea that if I do right and follow the rules, then good will happen. And my life will be easy, comfortable, and convenient.

My friend Alice summarized this feeling: "I wish that I could go back and tell myself that God gives all of the good things out of grace and all of the difficult things aren't because we did something wrong. But sometimes God leads us through difficult things because he's using them to shape us. I don't know if God made Milly to have autism or if that is a result of living in a fallen world. That's something that I question every day. But I do know that the struggles she has, more than anything else, have shaped our family in a way that I think brings glory to God. Way more than the easy, fun, and good things ever could."[1]

I had to ask myself, "Why do I want a different child? What am I hoping to gain?" The list easily comes to mind: ease, acceptance, achievement. Here's the good news: God can handle my wrestling. Like Job asking, "Why did I not die at birth, come out from the womb and expire?" (Job 3:11 ESV), or Habakkuk asking, "How long, LORD, must I call for help, but you do not listen?" (Hab. 1:2). Wrestling means you are embracing, not rejecting God. In her book *Amazed and Confused*, Heather Zempel observed, "As Habakkuk embraced God's character, he was forced to wrestle with God's actions; and as he wrestled with God's actions, he embraced His character."[2]

In the moments my heart wants a different situation or child, I can embrace God's sovereign, all-knowing character. Instead of annoyingly asking, "Why did You give me *this* child?" I can ask, "Why did You give *me* this child? How will You use him or her to shape and mold our family for Your good purposes?"

Walls Will Fall

An elevator button.

That's all it took for my four-year-old to firmly plant his green LEGO crocs as we walked from the gym into the parking garage. My attempts to explain how level 1A had already been pushed fell on deaf ears. He just kept repeating, "I don't want to go home. I don't want to go home . . ."

I stood there feeling helpless, with a two-year-old on my hip and a six-year-old venturing out toward our car. If he were my only child, I would have scooped him right up, carried him to the car, and worked things out when he was calm. But setting my two-year-old down to walk where cars kept zooming around the corner so I could pick up the statued son? Yeah, that wouldn't be the wisest solution.

I finally went right up to him, calmly told him all the trouble he was in, took his hand (firmly), and started walking. His chant became fiercer and stronger: "I don't want to go home. . . ." His refusals were common: "I don't want to go to school." "I don't want to go to church." "I don't want to eat spaghetti." I don't want to . . ." (heck, he was the one who didn't want to come out of the womb . . . laboring for a solid week, my large body sent home twice from the hospital because he wasn't ready yet).

Thankfully, my friend Tricia Goyer gave me a new perspective, one that kept me going when I wanted to give up. She said, "View the walls around his heart like the walls of Jericho. Keep circling them, believe God that the walls will fall."[3] I knew this child had a tender, caring heart. Perhaps his behaviors were acting like stubborn stone walls surrounding and protecting his kind heart. I had heard the stronger a child's will, the more sensitive the child.

My focus shifted when I made this realization. Instead of wanting to change who he was, I decided to communicate I'm on his team, because a harsher approach only strengthened his defense. Like Joshua advising the men who walked around the walls of Jericho, "Do not give a war cry, do not raise your voices, do not say a word until the day I tell you to shout. Then shout!" (Josh. 6:10).

I'm pretty forgetful. Just two years before, I'd come to a similar conclusion with my other challenging boy. He was frequently disobeying at home and at school, purposefully hurting his brothers, crossing well-established boundaries, and creating unnecessary stress in our home. Our response had been to increase the strength of those boundaries by removing privileges and ignoring purposeful, attention-getting behaviors. All the things professionals tell you to do. But it didn't work.

Thankfully I shared my concerns with my boy-mom mentor, Leslie. She directed me to read a particular chapter from *Seasons of a Mother's Heart*, by Sally Clarkson. I read words that I could have written:

> Every time he tested my patience, I responded by becoming even more strict than I had been the last time. Somehow, I had convinced myself that this increased harshness in discipline was the only appropriate response to his decreasing efforts at obedience. If he would not control himself, I reasoned, then I would control him.[4]

I was frustrated like Sally. The approach she and I were trying did not work. I needed something different. Attempting to control him with behavior-modification techniques was not working. With Sally's help I realized he needed an inside-out approach. Instead of focusing on his behavior, I needed to connect with his heart.

Inside Out

The first step in working from the inside out was to study who God made him to be. I took a step back and evaluated what made this little guy tick. I discovered the following:

- He is extremely relational (his words: "I don't like to be alone") and an extrovert (getting energy from being with others).
- He desires to please and gain approval.
- He is persistent in getting what he wants . . . even if it requires breaking a rule.
- He wants any kind of attention (positive or negative).

In studying him I realized he has some great qualities that will serve him well as an adult. Those are attributes I didn't want to change. Instead of breaking him, I needed to work with these traits to help him become the person God intended for him to be. "God did not make a mistake in giving your child his or her personality, so don't make the mistake of being critical of it. Learn to appreciate God's handiwork in each of your children."[5]

Unfortunately, after studying my son, I realized he needed even more than the twenty minutes a day of one-on-one Mommy Time to get his "love tank" filled. (I actually don't think I've ever seen his love tank 100 percent filled!) One way I could give him the attention he craved in the midst of parenting other children and keeping up with my home was by having a positive and loving attitude when I interacted with him:

- smile more
- hug more
- listen more

This required a major heart shift. I remember reading this in Ann Voskamp's "10 Point Manifesto for Joyful Parenting": "Today, the moment when I am most repelled by a child's behavior, that is my sign to *draw the very closest to that child*."[6]

Part of drawing close was choosing to see that child how God sees him.

My friend Kelsey shared with me an idea she uses.[7] She prays and asks God for a vision of who He is creating her child to be. When she did this exercise, she imagined a beautiful light pink peony, giant and open. Then it closed really quickly into a bud. She saw herself prying open the petals one by one. God impressed upon her that she was interfering with the future blossoming. She needed to trust that her daughter would become that beautiful peony in His perfect timing. She said the peace she had after asking for that vision changed her daily parenting.

I remember getting feedback from a teacher about how one of my boys struggled to be self-controlled. She told me about his impulsivity and the negative impacts on the classroom. When I saw my son, all I could think was, *Why can't you be more self-controlled?*

I found myself nit-picking him, pointing out each time he acted without thinking. He and I were weary by bedtime, filled with discouragement and frustration.

The next morning, in my time with God, I asked Him why He didn't give me an easier child. Gently, God said, "I made him like that on purpose. I created him to be a mighty warrior who isn't self-controlled but jumps into battle without thinking. When I prompt him to move, I know he won't hesitate." How I saw my son changed. How I spoke to him changed. Instead of seeing him as a problem to be solved, I saw him as a person to be loved.

Holding on to this positive vision of his future self shifted our daily interactions. Even better, I spoke that identity over him, and he felt seen and loved instead of criticized and needing to change.

Have you ever asked God how He sees your kids? If you are discouraged by the behavior and character you see today, take a moment in prayer to ask God for a view into how He will develop your child. Then you will be armed with positive words to notice the uniqueness instead of continually criticizing what that child is doing wrong.

What makes your child unique? Is she more physical than verbal? Would he rather play alone than with friends? Does she struggle to follow directions?

Make a list of things that tend to be challenges. In a column next to that list, ask God to give you insight into how those differences could be future superpowers. Sally Clarkson shared with me a prayer she prayed over her outside-the-box son, Nathan, who has bipolar disorder and obsessive-compulsive disorder: "God, show me how to love the child You gave me and how to release him within his limitations and personality into this world as a healthy human being."[8]

Both of my outside-the-box boys were already a challenge at four years old. But they were only four years old! At this developmental stage, a child is becoming more aware of the outside world. Fears start increasing. For boys, some of this unrest shows up in less impulse control and more aggression. Pediatric counselor David Thomas told me that he treats more four- and fourteen-year-old boys than any other age.[9] He knows there is a testosterone surge at fourteen and wonders if there may be a similar situation happening at four years old. (Although doctors and researchers do not agree that a testosterone surge happens in the toddler years.)

No matter the cause, it was helpful for me to sympathize with my sons knowing it is a challenging stage for most boys. And if anyone should be comforting instead of criticizing him, I hope it's me.

Didn't God do that for me? In my "undesirable state," He lowered Himself to be born as a baby here on earth. Jesus walked in human flesh. He was a four-year-old boy. He is the ultimate sympathizer. "For we do not have a high priest who is unable to sympathize with our weaknesses, but one who in every respect has been tempted as we are, yet without sin" (Heb. 4:15 ESV).

Another gift David Thomas gave me was over chips and queso. He and Sissy Goff were in town for a speaking event at our boys' school. Afterward I took them to my favorite Mexican restaurant and maximized my time with two of my favorite childhood experts. I shared with David how my then nine-year-old boy had been acting—emotional explosions, retreating to his room, and struggling socially. Did we need to take him to a counselor, or what could we do to help?

David kindly encouraged me in this hard situation. He said, "I often wonder if the boys I see in counseling at thirteen and fourteen years old wouldn't need to come see me if they'd had one year of occupational therapy before hitting puberty." Counseling may be something he'll need in the future. But David suggested that the next right step would be to have him evaluated by an occupational therapist.

A month later we learned that this child who had been so strong-willed had actual neurological differences in how he processes vestibular and proprioceptive sensory information. For instance, after spinning he didn't have a typical eye movement response and never felt dizzy. His body is feeling the movement but his brain isn't registering it correctly. That mismatch causes him to feel "out of sorts" or dysregulated.

When a child is dysregulated, he or she can go into a fight-or-flight state to protect themselves. The behaviors we had been experiencing were his way to deal with a body that was constantly dysregulated. Occupational therapist Lynne Jackson says, "Imagine if the volume on all your sounds and the sensations in your body was turned up and you were trying to fall asleep, that would be really hard. Car rides and meals are often torturous. So then what are the kids doing? They're trying to cope. They're jumping down. They're complaining about the food and squirming in their seats. They're trying to do something so they feel in control."[10]

Fluctuations between regulation and dysregulation impact a child's ability to connect with others and learn new information. Licensed professional counselor and friend Charissa Fry helped me understand this concept better. She referred to the ideal learning zone as the "Window of Tolerance." When we are in the zone, we feel calm and can effectively process input. This phenomenon isn't isolated to kids. "If I am dysregulated, I cannot regulate my child. So if I'm in fight-or-flight and yelling at my child, there's no amount of yelling that brings him or her back into the window. And sometimes parents think the yelling is working, but what you're doing isn't getting your child in the window. They're going into collapse and into a place of fear."[11]

Instead of wanting easier kids or disconnecting through criticism, I've found it's best to let my hard-to-handle boys know I'm with them. I'll walk with them, praising God and waiting for the stubborn walls to fall. I don't know how many circles I will have to make, but eventually those walls will fall. "When the trumpets sounded, the army shouted, and at the sound of the trumpet, when the men gave a loud shout, the wall collapsed. . . . They devoted the city to the LORD" (Josh. 6:20–21).

The ultimate goal in our parenting isn't for easy kids to make us look good. It's for our children to surrender to the truth of who God is and allow Christ to rule their hearts. When that moment happens, trumpets will blare. The heavens will celebrate. Because God desires that more than we ever could.

It's only fitting that after capturing Jericho, the Israelites devoted the city to the Lord. The middle name of one of my boys is Corban, the Hebrew word meaning, "consecrated to God." It was a decision before he was born. Before I knew the challenges we would face. I know my heavenly Father desires all our boys to know and love Him and to serve Him wholeheartedly. He's the only one who can draw hearts to Himself. Given the strength of will I've seen in these boys, they are gonna make some mighty warriors of God.

One night as I tucked my son into bed, with a downcast face, he said, "I'm an idiot. I always mess up. Nobody wants to be my friend cuz I'm so dumb." Now I could have done the typical mom thing and told him, "Honey, that is not true. You are the smartest boy I know. And you have lots of friends."

Instead, I said, "I don't believe that to be true. It doesn't sound like what God thinks about you. Should we ask God?" He hesitantly nodded his head. "Okay, so we're gonna ask God what He thinks about you. We'll be still and listen to what He says. When something comes across your mind, we'll thank Him for how He sees you, okay?" Another slow nod.

After a minute of silence, I began to pray, "Lord, thank You that You see this boy as a caregiver . . ." I couldn't finish praying before my son's eyes popped open and he excitedly said, "That's what I heard too!"

May I continue to ask God how He sees my kids and who He created them to be. To release the desire to have kids who make me look good. And to embrace how God is transforming me as I love my outside-the-box children.

> **Isolating Idea**
> *I would be a better parent if I had different kids.*
>
> **Connecting Truth**
> *I am a better parent because of my kids' differences.*

Discussion Questions

1. Do you have a child who consistently gets in trouble at church/school/playdates? How do you respond when you get hard feedback about him or her?

2. Have you wrestled with God about your challenging child? What part of God's character helps you reconcile His actions?

3. Have you considered the gift behind the challenge in your child? How could that hard behavior be shaped to be a positive in the future?

4. If someone in your group has a child with a special need, ask them how that has impacted their other relationships. Has it made it harder to connect with other moms? How can you encourage that mom today?

5. Take a moment before or during your group time to pray and ask God to give you a vision for your challenging child.

6. How does learning about the "window of tolerance" affect how you will approach disagreements with your child in the future?

twelve

Do Like I Do

Since I didn't grow up in a Christian home, I often feel like I am many steps behind other moms when it comes to teaching my children about Jesus. I don't have the Bible stories and songs learned in Sunday school as a foundation. I grew up Jewish and had the Old Testament as my guide. The Old Testament is filled with a God who is wrathful, just, and holy. I missed out on the New Testament God of grace, mercy, and love. I want my kids to know God is just and holy but He's also mercy and grace—through Jesus.

—Lauren

At the end of a Friday after a long week, the very last thing a mom wants to do is correct another act of disobedience. But as I looked in the mirror to apply mascara, I happened to see my four-year-old son directly disobeying a request I had just made. Instead of ignoring it (which I wanted to do), I put the makeup down, took his hand, and led him into my walk-in closet.

175

He and I sat on the floor, his cuddly body wrapped in my arms, and we talked about disobedience. That's when he asked: "Mom, why does God want us to make bad choices?"

Oh, sweet son. That was never God's plan.

His plan was to walk alongside us in beautiful, peaceful communion. But then those first humans believed a lie and disobeyed a loving God. And we've been stuck with the ugliness ever since. God's plan was for us to live in shalom—peace, harmony, wholeness, health, blessing—with Him. But sin brought the disruption. Choosing our way over God's caused a separation between us and God.

Thankfully that's not the end of the story. Because He loved us so much, He couldn't leave us separated from Him. So He sent Jesus, His Son, to save us and make things right with God again.

"Mom, well, I believe in God."

"You do?" I replied with shock.

Less than two months earlier on the night before Easter, while lying side-by-side in his bed, this four-year-old told me he didn't believe God was real. In fact, I think he said he loved Satan (just to make his point clear), which made the current conversation so shocking.

"Yeah, and I believe in Jesus too."

"Wow! That's great. Do you believe Jesus came to rescue you from sin and make things right with God? That He died and rose again?"

"Yep."

Then another miracle as he prayed unprompted: "Dear Lord, thank You that You didn't want Adam and Eve to eat that fruit. Thank You that You never gave up on us. Thank You that You sent Jesus to die for my sin on the cross and He rose again. Amen."

His prayer began at a moment right when his two big brothers walked into the closet. We all witnessed walls fall! Remember the last chapter? Our faithful prayers for those Jericho walls to fall were answered just as quickly as back in Joshua's time. And we celebrated (and continue to celebrate) because only God can soften hard hearts. When I woke up on that Friday morning, seeing a long day at the end of a long week, there were no elaborate evangelism plans on my to-do list. But God had it scheduled on His calendar since before time began.

Therein lies the freedom. God is outside of time. He knows the exact moment a person will choose faith in Him. His desire is that all would choose Him, but he offers salvation as a gift. Some choose to open the gift, and others choose to walk away. That's the mixed blessing of free will.

As parents who follow Jesus, we long for our children to follow Him, yet we often feel ill-equipped and overwhelmed by the task. We fear we don't know the right things to say. Or maybe we'll say all the right things and still raise a prodigal, a child who intentionally chooses to walk away from God. (But let's not forget in the biblical account the prodigal son returned and was welcomed with open arms by his father.)

Perhaps you didn't grow up in a home where the Bible was read or God was discussed. You may feel insecure with no model to follow. Here's a piece of hope if you are feeling insecure about your lack of faith legacy. My parents were first-generation believers. Living a life of faith wasn't modeled for them. And yet God is the one who draws hearts to Himself. He shapes and forms us for His good purposes.

My father didn't grow up in a home with daily family devotionals. When he was a teenager his mom died suddenly, and my dad lost his way for a while. It took my mom discovering Christ through a neighborhood Bible study to introduce my dad to personal salvation. In his adult years he began studying, surrendering, and embracing the gift of grace.

By the time I was in elementary school, my dad was teaching two weekly Bible studies to businesspeople during their lunch breaks. Each morning before we started homeschool and he headed off to the law office, he gathered my brother and me around the kitchen table and led us through whatever book of the Bible he was studying at the time.

My mom also lived out the command, "Go and make disciples." First with her children, then with women she gathered in our home. Around that same holy kitchen table, she led them through the basic tenets of faith and spiritual disciplines like Bible study, prayer, and service. Well past my bedtime, I would often sneak down the stairs and peek around the doorway to watch her gracefully lead.

My parents didn't have a model to follow. But they had a God to lead them. Mentors who informed their faith. God's Word to instruct them on how to live His way. And the Holy Spirit to empower them to parent differently than they were parented. All of that is available to you as well.

Walking Alongside

If I close my eyes, I can still see how light patches dotted the wooded path. I can feel the tender grip of my dad's hand wrapped around mine. The gentle breeze blowing through the limbs above our heads.

Growing up in a house on five wooded acres, a walk like this was my norm. A norm I took for granted. Such a dreamy childhood to have all that space to explore, learn, and experience God's creation. And a father who took the time to enjoy it with me.

With so many memories made in those magical woods, my mind easily recalls one specific walk. My dad had stopped and pointed to a vine winding around a tree. As his fingers traced the serpentine plant, he easily quoted, "I am the vine; you are the branches. If you remain in me and I in you, you will bear much fruit; apart from me you can do nothing" (I don't think he quoted the address, but if you're wondering it's John 15:5).

He then pointed to a stick on the ground. Dry, brittle, lifeless compared to the vibrant, green vine—illustrating how our fruitfulness is directly related to our connection to the source. Without being attached to Christ, our life source, production is dry, brittle, and lifeless.

Though the vine Jesus referenced was probably weighed down with grapes, this Indiana version proved a sufficient substitute. The concept of "abiding" was never forgotten because of a shared experience with a beloved instructor, my dad. Jesus understood the power of physical illustrations and using items from the environment to teach truth.

Mary DeMuth, author of the book *Building the Christian Family You Never Had*, shared with me how Jesus would *peripateo* with his disciples.[1] This Greek word means "walking around." He would *peripateo* with them, asking questions along the way. Like my father with me, Mary went on walks with her kids, engaging them in open dialogue. Choosing to respond without overreacting to anything they shared with her. And she, in turn, would authentically share her brokenness and weaknesses. Asking for forgiveness if she'd wronged them in any way. Is there a better way to teach our children about sin and grace than pointing it out in their parents' lives?

This idea of walking alongside each other in faith isn't just a nice concept in theory; it is backed by research. In my interview with Fuller Seminary professor and practical theology researcher Dr. Kara Powell, she said, "One of the things that surprised me in our research is that when young people feel close to their parents, they're also more open to what's important to their parents, including their faith."[2]

In previous chapters we've discussed the importance of connecting to God in our own lives, spending time reading Scripture, listening to the Lord, and praying God's Word. That is our abiding in the vine. Influencing the strength of connection we have to God.

Then there is the warmth of relationship that our kids have to us. This is the connection aspect I wrote about in the chapter on discipline. Here are a few more thoughts on that from Dr. Powell:

> Multiple studies have shown how important it is that kids are connected to their parents—heart-to-heart connection. And what's a little daunting is that it's not how I feel connected to my kids that counts. *It's how connected my kids feel to me.* And our kids are often harsher graders on that. So we might feel pretty connected with our kids, but our kids might not be feeling the same in return, and that's what really matters.[3]

Although worrying about how my kids perceive our connection could be intimidating, when I heard this from Dr. Powell, I may have actually sighed with a bit of relief.

Anyone else have the idea that "good Christian families" sit around the dinner table and exegetically study Scripture? Or maybe sing hymns together by the fireplace? At the bare minimum, I imagine they have regular family devotions, during which each child adds thoughtful insights.

Despite my repeated attempts, we've never been that family. In fact, when I've tried to orchestrate moments like these, my efforts to manufacture a "spiritual experience" often remove any warmth from the room. Threats get thrown around. Reading verses like, "Love one another as Christ loved you" through clenched teeth is the definition of hypocritical.

Once again, my family benefits when I toss out the ideal and settle into what works best for us. We're a tactile family. Snuggling during worship services works better for us than forcing my kids to keep their hands to themselves in church. Cuddling in bed reading a Bible story feels better than trying to keep all four boys quiet during formal family devotions. Nuzzling my nose into a little one's neck while I pray has become the nightly ritual.

In fact, measuring the *warmth* of faith training moments matters more to me now than measuring up to an unrealistic standard.

My hope is to help other parents have the same realization. To help foster healthy relationships that lead to lasting faith. Instead of parents forcing kids to be "good Christians" and in the process driving a wedge between them and their kids and not attaining their goal.

Worth Doing Badly

Several moms have reached out to me frustrated that their husbands aren't leading their family spiritually. I understand that frustration. For many years I wished Bruce took more initiative to lead our family in prayer and Bible study. To bring up God in conversations.

A couple of things encouraged me not to let our reality keep me from teaching our boys. The first was a conversation with Jen Wilkin, popular Bible study author and teacher.[4] She challenged me to expand the definition of a "spiritual leader." Having been raised by a single mom, there wasn't a man in her home to act as the spiritual leader. But that didn't stop her mom from fervently praying for Jen and for God to grow big in her life.

Like I shared earlier, we often have this idea that the husband leads the family through devotionals each night. In Jen's marriage they decided to lean into one another's spiritual gifts. Instead of putting the burden of Bible teaching on her husband, she embraces her skills by teaching God's Word to her kids. And her husband leads the family spiritually in other ways.

The other helpful insight came from one of my favorite resources on the topic of guiding our children's faith called *Revolutionary Parenting*, by George Barna. The Barna Group conducted studies of adults who had grown up in homes of faith. They looked for environmental similarities in those who are now deemed "Spiritual Champions," which they defined as "an irrepressible follower of Jesus Christ who accepts the Bible as truth, lives by its principles, and seeks ways to impact the world and continually deepen his or her relationship with God." They found in their research that raising a spiritual champion "is best accomplished by having at least one parent in the home who is fully committed to honoring God through his or her parenting practices."[5]

One parent committed. That's all. If you are that parent, take courage. You do not have to wait for your spouse to get his act together (or he doesn't have to wait for you). My favorite biblical example of a mother leading her child to know Christ is found in 2 Timothy 1:5. Paul is writing to Timothy and he is reminded of Timothy's "sincere faith, which first lived in your grandmother Lois and in your mother Eunice."

The Barna Group also said, "These Revolutionary Parents use a lot of 'God talk'—not empty phrases, but a genuine intermingling of their relationship with God and their daily experiences and choices."[6] Everyday moments interpreted through a spiritual lens. Like the familiar Deuteronomy 6:7: "Impress them on your children. Talk about them when you sit at home and when you walk along the road, when you lie down and when you get up."

When I was young, after watching movies, my parents asked us questions about how the film aligned with what we believe about God and read in His Word. We'd discuss character flaws and how wrong choices panned out. Of course, every story has a redemptive arc, which we would point out reminds us of Christ's redeeming work in our lives.

Starting today you can learn alongside your children. It is not too late. Your kids are not too old. If you are breathing while reading this book, God will take what you offer in faith and multiply it. Even pray, "I believe, help my unbelief." The goal is not perfection. In fact, several parents have shared with me that it was sharing their failures and asking for forgiveness that most helped their children understand grace.

Sometimes we sabotage the good in pursuit of the great. I'm not the first to point that out. French writer Voltaire quoted an Italian proverb: "The best is the enemy of the good."[7] Philosophers for centuries have counseled against the pursuit of perfectionism. We know we shouldn't, but we often put good things on hold until we can do them perfectly.

Around 2013, I decided not to wait for my husband to lead us in family devotions. Having read several books by Sally Clarkson, I was inspired by her to have teatime with my boys—because formal tea is not just for moms and daughters. One time my mother-in-law joined us during one of those teatimes and came up with a fun way to present the teatime goodies. Looking through the pantry, she found some graham crackers that she separated into four rectangles. Then she sliced a banana into bite-sized pieces. "Everything feels more special when you cut it into pieces," she said with a wink.

I keep our teas in a wooden hinged box. Letting each boy choose a tea was part of the whole experience. Before sitting down at the table, one boy would pick a children's Bible from the basket we keep in the living room. Another boy would flip through it and pick a story to read. Lastly, we would decide how many graham crackers and banana slices each boy would get. As they nibbled on treats and sipped tea, I read God's words to them. What amazed me were the many times a five-minute story turned into a thirty-minute conversation. They would ask a question about something in the story, which sometimes led us to another story.

I wouldn't trade those teatimes for anything in the world. They were imperfectly perfect. There was no regularity to them besides doing them whenever we felt like it. Yet often enough that my teenage boys still remember.

The memory of similar times with my dad will never be lost. Instead of teatime, we went on donut dates. I'd order a sprinkled donut and chocolate milk. We'd crack open my Precious Moments Bible and study together. Then he'd listen to my tender, little-girl heart, empathizing with whatever I found challenging at the time. We'd end that holy time with prayer.

Another faith tool my parents modeled often was spontaneous prayer. Yes, we would pray before meals (still feels odd if I don't pray before eating). But they would also start praying if we saw an ambulance. Or if we were trying to decide what to do as a family, we would stop and pray.

Watching my parents imperfectly seek God on small and big life matters made it easy for me to do the same. Prayer wasn't intimidating. We were simply communicating with God. Letting the Holy Spirit groan on our behalf if we didn't know exactly what to say.

If you've never prayed with your kids because you've been afraid of saying the wrong thing, I want to encourage you at some point in the next twenty-four hours to invite your kids to pray with you. Begin with God's name, include something you are thankful for, ask God for help with whatever you need, and then finish with "Amen." Not only will you feel supernatural peace through the practice of prayer, but you will model to your child that he or she can offer similar requests to God. In the Old Testament, only the high priest could enter the Holy of Holies to be in God's presence. With His death on the cross, Jesus bought us full access to God. So we can communicate with Him freely at any moment. It would be a travesty if such a beautiful gift went underutilized.

No Junior Holy Spirit

"Were robbers ever little kids?" my second son asks from the back seat.

"Yes, everyone was once a little kid."

"What?" he questioned with complete shock and horror. "How could a bad guy once be a nice kid? What makes a kid want to be a robber?"

"Well, it depends on how that child grew up. Maybe no one ever told him there is another way to do things. Maybe a mommy never told him to be kind and share. Maybe he knows the difference between right and wrong but doesn't care if he gets in trouble. Or maybe he's just desperate."

"What does it mean to be desperate?"

"If he doesn't have any money and his family needs to eat, he may steal food to feed his family . . . kind of like Jean Valjean in *Les Mis*."

"Oh, tell me about Jean Valjean again."

Yes, I have told my boys the story of *Les Misérables*, at least a simplified version. About Jean Valjean's imprisonment for stealing a loaf of bread and then being set free but to a lifetime parole. How a priest invited him in for food and rest and Valjean returned that kindness by stealing silver in the middle of the night. But when the police caught Valjean and brought him back to the priest, the priest claimed he gave Valjean the silver, only he had forgotten to take the candlesticks. Grace in action. Undeserved favor. A simple encouragement to start a new life. To make things right.

"Valjean decided to start over. To choose to do right. To accept the priest's invitation. In doing so he changed his name."

"Like Saul changed to Paul? Or like how Batman's friend changed from 'Row' to 'Robin'?"

"Ha, yeah, kind of. Though I don't think Robin ever changed his name."

Little did Price know, but at the time I felt like we should start calling him by another name. From challenging to charming. From frustrating to fabulous. From stressful to enjoyable.

Just a year before, when he was four years old, I had struggled with his strong will and applied the "inside-out approach" I mentioned in the last chapter to help with his difficult behavior.

I wish I could remember some grand conversion conversation. A moment he said, "Mommy, I'm ready to pray," like I had for his younger brother. But I know he surrendered his life to Christ at some point because we were seeing the fruit of his faith.

A spiritual tenderness had grown in Price. He always had a sweet heart, always the first to rush in and offer help. What we saw change was a desire to know God more. A thirst to really understand the heart of God and know the stories in His Word. For Easter that year, we'd given him a copy of *The Action Bible*. I kept finding him bent over it, studying its pages, even though he couldn't read yet!

When a child confesses a belief that Jesus paid the price of sin with His death on the cross and then defeated the power of sin through His resurrection, that child receives the Holy Spirit. And according to this verse, "In him you also, when you heard the word of truth, the gospel of your salvation, and believed in him, were sealed with the promised Holy Spirit" (Eph. 1:13 ESV), a believer is "sealed" with the Holy Spirit until the second coming of Christ when salvation is made complete.

On the flip side, a child doesn't receive the Holy Spirit until confessing faith. So, I can't expect that child to demonstrate the fruit of the Spirit of love, joy, peace, patience, kindness, goodness, gentleness, self-control. Have you ever considered that? Your preschooler who is challenging you now has a sin nature that is not controlled by the Holy Spirit. Perhaps he or she needs some extra prayers, am I right?

This is one of the greatest ways to not mom alone. To have God's presence in your child. Convicting from the inside what you are instructing on the outside. Because there is no junior Holy Spirit. The same Spirit in me is present in my child after professing faith. Together we are one Spirit.

I found that with each profession of faith in our family, working together as a team became a whole lot easier. Yes, we are still sinners in need of grace, but sin has no power over us. We have been set free from the law of sin and death and are led by the Spirit. For this reason, if your children are still little, pray specifically for salvation at a young age—to follow Christ with his or her whole heart.

One fantastic parenting tool I discovered is the book *Praying the Scriptures for Your Children*, by Jodie Berndt. In it she explains the power of praying God's Word back to Him, particularly when it comes to issues of parenting. When Jodie came on the podcast, she said, "We know that He is a loving God who knows our needs and our kids' needs better than we know them. So when we lift our children to Him and surrender them, He's going to do for them what He knows they need. It might not be necessarily in the timing or the ways that He would've ordained, but in Isaiah 55 it says that His ways are higher and better than our ways. When we come to believe that, it can really bring peace to our lives."[8]

In Jodie's book, each chapter addresses a different area of parenting and provides Scripture prompts to pray. (Bonus: she has an edition for parents of teens and another for parents of adult children.) I love her prayer for our children to come to know God at a young age:

> Heavenly Father . . . Open [their] eyes and turn them from darkness to light, and from the power of Satan to God, so that they may receive forgiveness of sins and a place among those who are sanctified by faith in Christ.
>
> Acts 26:18[9]

Speaking of God's Word, have you ever felt like it would be good to memorize with your kids but felt incredibly intimidated by the idea? Raising my hand! I remember memorizing verses at church or as part of my Christian school. But how could I help my boys hide God's Word in their heart without making it a painful or legalistic process?

When my oldest was around eight years old, I discovered the book *The Well-Versed Family*, by Caroline Boykin. Caroline shared how a sibling battle over a Barbie doll led her to start memorizing Scripture with her girls. It prompted her to figure out a way to link memory verses to everyday experiences.

I remember one activity from her book involved offering my boys a twenty-dollar bill. I wrote out on our chalkboard the verse: "For there is one God and one mediator between God and mankind, the man Christ Jesus" (1 Tim. 2:5). Then I followed Caroline's instruction: "Take a moment and explain what the word 'mediator' means (in this verse: 'one who mediates between two parties with a view of producing peace' or a 'go-between'). . . . Ask your kids, how many 'Gods' does this verse say there are? How many 'mediators' between God and men are there? Who is the mediator?"[10]

We had a great conversation. Even talked about when you buy something at the store, the storekeeper is the mediator between the person who made the item and you, the buyer. Then I walked them over to the stairs (again, Caroline Boykin's idea). I told them to pretend that at the top of the stairs is "heaven" where God lives. In order to get the twenty dollars, they had to figure out a way to get to the top of the stairs under these conditions:

Don't touch the stairs.

Don't touch the walls.

Don't touch the railings.

Don't bring anything with them.

It was fun to watch their little minds spin trying to come up with the best way to get to the top. My four-year-old threw himself toward the stairs in an attempt to jump all the way. After tossing around some ideas, my six-year-old said, "We need Jesus. We could pray for him to carry us up to the top." He got it . . . kind of. So I put him on my back and carried him up the stairs. To earn the twenty dollars, all they had to do was ask me to carry them to the top.

For salvation, to reconcile ourselves to God, we need to rely on our mediator, Jesus. We can't force our way. There is nothing we can do for ourselves. We must rely completely on the work of Jesus to gain access to our heavenly Father. My hope is through this activity the verse would be etched in their hearts and the truth of the gift of salvation would be made real to them.

(A few tips: you don't have to have stairs to use this activity. Designate a room or the couch to be "heaven." Be ready for some grumbling if no one earns the twenty dollars. Maybe offer ice cream instead and at the end talk about the activity while eating ice cream together. Enjoy the precious thoughts of your little ones. I loved when my four-year-old got to the top of the stairs and in his excitement said, "It *is* heaven! See!" and pointed to light shining into the hallway from a bedroom window.)

The Whole Body

Biblical community begins with the Trinity (Father, Son, and Holy Spirit). To reflect God's communal image, Jesus led His followers to be in faith communities. Paul reminded early believers (and us) that we are "one body" (1 Cor. 12:9). It's clear, though, that God intends for parents to be the primary faith instructors to their kids. Dr. Kara Powell encourages us, "The good news is parenting is not meant to be a solo sport. God has designed us to live in community. God's designed us to be in teams and be in friendships."[11]

It's a bit humbling as I start thinking about all the people God provided to disciple my boys alongside us. Whether it's been through formal programming or sovereign provision, we've been blessed with an abundance of believers in our community. A bulk of that community has come from partnering with our local church body.

According to Barna research, "Unlike parents who embrace the 'dump and run' strategy of spiritual nurturing—dump the kids at church, run off until the allotted time has expired, then wait until next week to repeat the process to provide their offspring with their dose of spiritual experiences—Revolutionary Parents see their church as an invaluable partner in a long-term effort to raise a mature follower of Christ."[12]

There was a season when several of our good friends decided to leave our church. The primary reason was their kids' dissatisfaction with the children's ministry programming. While I completely believe guiding our children's faith is important, I also know that my kids are fickle fans. From week to week, they can express different opinions about teachers, administrators, or programs. I also know that their faith is not 100 percent dependent on their church experience. I believe it benefits my children when we model staying in a faith community not based on how well it serves us but on how we serve.

In that season when our friends started attending a different church, we decided to stay but shake things up. Instead of going to their assigned Sunday school class, my older two boys began serving in the four-year-old class. That small decision made a huge impact in their lives.

One of the primary leaders of that class, Miss Nancy, is a prayer warrior and godly woman (who, as I mentioned earlier, happened to be in a Bible study with my mom decades before). Her joyful spirit and dedication to God's Word seeped into my boys' hearts. She encouraged my boys in how they led the little ones. Instead of getting in trouble for distracting behavior in their own classrooms, they found identity and worth through teaching and serving.

Another unique way God provided spiritual mentors for my boys is through family camp. For seven summers our family has gone to Pine Cove Camp in Tyler, Texas. Through costumed theme nights and silly games, dedicated college students minister to our family. By seeing older guys serving others, for God's glory, my boys keep their eyes fixed on a goal. They want to be just like those counselors. My hope is that goal will get them through the challenging teen years where missteps can have life-long consequences.

I've also heard about the value in having four or five adults your child can go to when they have faith questions. We've fostered those relationships a couple of ways. One way is through our small group. As I shared in chapter 3, we started meeting once a month for a Shabbat dinner. Before we sit down to eat, we say a blessing over each of our kids. In the future, we would like to trade off and speak a blessing over our friends' kids, letting them know that there are other adults who see their gifts and believe God will use them for His glory.

Another way is through an annual mother-son program called "God's Mighty Warriors." It was started by my friend Sara when my boys were preschoolers to help support our boys as they grow into men. Each summer, we'd gather one day a week, with a different mom in charge of a lesson and activity each time. It was a way to anchor our summer, especially in the years with young boys, when we had lots of time and very little structure. Having one day a week planned out helped me relax on the other days.

Typically, during the spring, the moms involved would get together for dinner and pick a theme and activities and assign duties. Over ten years, we've covered a variety of topics: the armor of God, Jesus's life and ministry, heroes of the Bible, parables, living out our faith, and many others. And we've made a whole lot of memories. My boys have friendships with boys in other schools and churches. They also have other moms who speak into their lives. Even better, in the teenage years, Sara has brought in godly men to teach and mentor the boys.

I share these things not as a prescription for how you need to guide your child spiritually, but as examples of different ways you can invite others into the discipleship process. As Paul David Tripp says, "That's the legacy of 10,000 conversations that God has used to progressively alter the content of that child's heart. You've got to look down the road. Change is seldom an event. It's almost always a process. Jesus bears the burden of spiritual welfare for our children. He is in me, He is for me, and He is with me."[13]

May we recognize the ultimate way to not mom alone is for our children to be followers of Christ—God's presence in them.

> ## Isolating Idea
> *I don't know how to lead my kids to Jesus.*
>
> ## Connecting Truth
> *I walk in faith with my kids and let others fill in the gaps.*

Discussion Questions

1. What is your personal testimony? Have any of your children professed faith in Jesus?
2. Who taught you how to pray and read God's Word when you became a believer? How comfortable do you feel walking alongside your child on his or her faith journey?
3. Who is the spiritual leader in your home? What does that look like for your family?
4. What are the implications for our kids if we understand that there is no Junior Holy Spirit?
5. What programs or people come alongside you as you disciple your kids' faith? Is there anything you've been wanting to do, or are there people you've been wanting to invite to help you?

Acknowledgments

Bruce—I can't imagine mothering these four boys without your humor, joy, organizational skills, and cleaning ability. Thank you for willingly taking charge of our crew so I could go write in quiet. Thank you for acknowledging the hard parts of motherhood while reminding me that I'm doing a great job. Thank you for encouraging me to use my gifts in writing online, starting the podcast, and launching this book. You're my favorite walking buddy.

My boys—Quade, Price, Watts, and Knox—thank you for helping me care less about what other people think. Thank you for giving me abundant grace as we grow together. Thank you for all the love, cuddles, and laughter. You are unique, godly men in the making. Y'all are my favorites.

Mom—thank you for modeling for me that a woman can be strong and also supported by her community. Thank you for guiding my faith in how you seek God through His Word and in prayer. Thank you for lifting me up every day when you talk to God.

DadDad and MomMom—Bruce and Rosemary—thank you for faithfully following Christ and modeling a godly marriage to your children. Thank you for always welcoming the outsider with joy and grace. Thank you for loaning your new home so I could have a quiet space to think and write during the COVID-19 quarantine. And thank you for leading and loving your son to be the best husband and dad ever!

My original Fam—Andrea, Scott, John, Jana, Adam—thank you for loving your Sissy well despite the physical distance. Thank you for encouraging me to keep going with the ministry God has given me.

Sisters from another mister—Sherri, Debbie, and Christina—thank you for adopting me into your sisterhood (even though you weren't so sure I was worthy of your bro in the beginning). You shaped a great guy in your brother, Bruce. It's been quite a ride parenting all these kiddos alongside one another. You have definitely helped me not mom alone!

Leslie Johnson—thank you for inviting me to your MomHeart group all those years ago. Thank you for helping me see the beauty in mothering four boys. Thank you for coaching me through this book-writing process. I would have quit at least three times without your guidance. Thank you most of all for inspiring me that my best years are still ahead of me as I watch you gracefully own your life.

The Best Small Group—Amber and Aaron Lee, Kari and Tommy Simpson, Abbey and Chris Carter—thank you for helping me process my feelings about writing a book. For watching me cry (a lot) and encouraging me to keep going.

Mastermind Girls—Kat Lee, Amy Lynn Andrews, Chrystal Evans Hurst, Elizabeth Griffin, Francie Winslow, Katie Orr, Lara Williams, Stacey Thacker—truly no words. You are my original internet people. We've been through a lot of life (and death) together. There honestly would be no blog or podcast or book without your love, support, and ministry expertise. Thank you for having my back always.

Legaclick—John and Jae Carpenter, Alan and Kathryn Morris, Randy and Megan Evans—thank you for believing in me enough to jokingly rename my ministry "Mother of God." Thank you for the laughter and memories and for keeping me grounded in grace.

The original playgroup—Erin Morgan, Pamela Garcia, Carrie Cassell, and Holly Ramsey—you mean more to me than you will ever know. Y'all were my first mom crew. You helped me navigate the terrifying waters of rearing tiny humans. Thank you for your consistent love, grace, encouragement, and wisdom.

Providence Praying Moms—Molly Rhodes, Kelsey Phillips, Allison Ryan, Shannon Copeland, Candace Crofford, Julie Rhodes— y'all's dedication to prayer shaped my personal prayer ministry. Thank you for asking God for vision about this book and encouraging me with blessing prayer.

Younger mom friends Hailey Bain, Stacey McCabe, Meredith Woodruff, Aubrie Norman, Angel Ricchuiti, Brittany Turner—you keep me relevant and held up with your faithful prayers.

Stephanie Tomba—thank you for frequently reminding me how God sees me and that I am one of the cool kids.

Neil and Vela Tomba—thank you for leading our church community with humility and grace. And for loaning me your home for a quiet day of writing.

Juleeta Harvey—thank you for believing in me when I didn't think I could write a book. And for letting me use your home while y'all were out of town. For seeing me when I was "not myself" and commiserating as the sole female in an all-male home.

Nick and Angela Kennedy—thank you both for investing in this journey. Nick, without skipping a beat you gave me your Apple pen and your encouragement to write. Angela, thank you for being my creative-process cheerleader.

Andrea Miller, Lisa Henry, Misty Persefield, Elizabeth Pounds, and Christine Gordon—thank you for helping me navigate the challenges of the school-age years. For processing the heartaches, new territories, and how to pick up four kids from three different carpools.

Pine Cove Bluffs Week Seven Families—there are no words for the love and support you've given our family for nearly a decade.

Your love, though we're apart for fifty-one weeks a year, has sustained us.

My "made-up" Dallas Board of Directors—Courtney DeFeo, Cari Trotter, Charity Reeb, Andrea Howey, Kay Wyma—thank you for brainstorming, crying, and creating by my side.

God's Mighty Warriors mamas—Sara Farrington, Kris Habashy, Heather Lipscomb, Brooke West, Miriam Sperring—thank you for helping me faithfully lead my little boys to become mighty men of God.

Sarah-Jane Menefee and Rachael Jamison—thank you for being queens of the details. For keeping the podcast running smoothly while I worked on the book. Thank you for your constant encouragement and presence in this ministry.

Revell Team—Andrea Doering, Rachel McRae, Mackenzie Gibor, Kristin Adkinson, Wendy Wetzel, Eileen Hanson, Erin Bartels, Olivia Peitsch, Sarah Traill, and Laura Palma—thank you for making this book a reality.

My agent, Jana Burson—you believed I could do it.

Preface

1. Vivek H. Murthy, MD, *Together: The Healing Power of Human Connection in a Sometimes Lonely World* (New York: HarperCollins, 2020), 9.

Chapter 1 Let Him Be a Jerk

1. Melody Beattie, *Codependent No More: How to Stop Controlling Others and Start Caring for Yourself* (Center City, MN: Hazelden, 1986), 64.

2. Beattie, *Codependent No More*, 84.

3. Jennie Allen (@jenniesallen), Instagram, October 1, 2020, https://www.instagram.com/p/CF0xklRjpCm.

4. For more information about Kat Lee's Hello Mornings ministry, go to https://www.hellomornings.org.

5. Jeannie Cunnion, *Mom Set Free—Bible Study Book: Good News for Moms Who are Tired of Trying to be Good Enough* (Nashville: Lifeway, 2017), 126.

6. Justin Hart, "If Half of Your Marketing Dollars Are Wasted You Should Be Shot," *Vunela*, March 30, 2017, https://magazine.vunela.com/if-half-of-your-marketing-dollars-are-wasted-you-should-be-shot-c1f505c1e56d.

Chapter 2 Mother of the Year

1. *The Princess Bride*, directed by Rob Reiner (Los Angeles: Twentieth Century Fox, 1987).

2. Graham Cooke, "The Nature of God," *Brilliant House Books* (YouTube video), July 19, 2013, https://www.youtube.com/watch?v=2pVyFCoKGBM.

3. A. W. Tozer, *The Pursuit of God* (Harrisburg, PA: Christian Publications, 1948), 105–6, emphasis added.

Chapter 3 Hole in My Bucket

1. Joanna Weaver, "9 Verses to Remind You—Jesus Understands," from *Having a Mary Heart in a Martha World*, January 11, 2017, https://joannaweaverbooks.com/2017/01/11/9-verses-remind-jesus-understands.

2. Katie Sherrod, "Fighting for the Family," episode 33, *Don't Mom Alone*, audio podcast, July 28, 2014, https://dontmomalone.com/2014/07/28/fighting-for-the-family-katie-sherrod-ep-33/.

3. Sally Lloyd-Jones, *The Jesus Storybook Bible: Every Story Whispers His Name* (Grand Rapids: Zondervan, 2007), 36.

4. The Trinity Forum, "Trinity Forum Readings: Theory of Moral Sentiments," accessed April 27, 2021, https://www.ttf.org/product/theory-of-moral-sentiments/.

5. Ruth Haley Barton, *Sacred Rhythms: Arranging Our Lives for Spiritual Transformation* (Downers Grove, IL: InterVarsity, 2006).

6. Dr. Saundra Dalton-Smith, "Which Type of Rest Do You Need?," episode 209, *Don't Mom Alone*, audio podcast, June 4, 2018, https://dontmomalone.com/2018/06/04/which-type-of-rest-do-you-need-saundra-dalton-smith-ep-209.

Chapter 4 Seeing Is Believing

1. Murthy, *Together*, 8.

2. Sara Hagerty, "When You Feel Unseen," episode 175, *Don't Mom Alone*, audio podcast, September 4, 2017, https://dontmomalone.com/2017/09/04/when-you-feel-unseen-sara-hagerty-ep-175.

3. Francis Chan, *Forgotten God: Reversing Our Tragic Neglect of the Holy Spirit* (Colorado Springs: David C. Cook, 2009).

4. HELPS Word-Studies, s.v. "phronema," *The Discovery Bible*, https://biblehub.com/greek/5427.htm.

5. Kelsey Phillips, "Listening to the Lord," episode 279, *Don't Mom Alone*, audio podcast, March 30, 2020, https://dontmomalone.com/2020/03/30/listening-to-the-lord-kelsey-phillips-ep-279.

6. Phillips, "Listening to the Lord."

Chapter 5 No Mom Is an Island

1. Shauna Niequist, "How to Get Real and Savor More," episode 65, *Don't Mom Alone,* audio podcast, March 23, 2015, https://dontmomalone.com/2015/03/23/how-to-get-real-savor-more-shauna-niequest-ep-65.

2. Pete Scazzero, "Unhurrying with a Rule of Life: A Long Form Interview with Pete Scazzero," interviewed by John Mark Comer, Bridgetown Church, audio podcast, January 7, 2020, https://bridgetown.church/teaching/unhurrying-with-a-rule-of-life/a-long-form-interview-with-pete-scazzero.

3. Niequist, "How to Get Real and Savor More."

4. John Townsend, PhD, *Boundaries DVD Facilitator Guide,* CloudTownsend.com, 2012, http://www.cloudtownsend.com/wp-content/uploads/2012/08/Boundaries-New-Revised-DVD-Facilitator-Guide_-Revised0812.pdf.

5. J. D. Douglas, ed., *New Bible Dictionary,* 2nd ed. (Downers Grove, IL: InterVarsity, 1982), 108.

Chapter 6 Cleaning Muddy Purses

1. C. S. Lewis, *Mere Christianity* (New York: Macmillan, 1952), preface.

2. Compiled and adapted by Rajneesh Nagda, Patricia Gurin, Jacyln Rodriguez, and Kelly Maxwell (2008), based on Diana Kardia and Todd Sevig, "Differentiating Dialogue from Discussion" (handout for the Program on Intergroup Relations, Conflict, and Community, University of Michigan, 1997); and Shelley Berman, "Comparing Dialogue and Debate" (paper based on discussions of the Dialogue Group of the Boston Chapter of Educators for Social Responsibility, 1998).

3. Dr. Alan Loy McGinnis, *The Friendship Factor: How to Get Closer to the People You Care For* (Minneapolis: Augsburg, 1979), 114.

4. Dee Brestin, *The Friendships of Women: Harnessing the Power in Our Heartwarming, Heartrending Relationships* (Colorado Springs: David C. Cook, 1988), 120.

5. Lynn Hoffman, "How to Have Healthy Conflict," episode 307, *Don't Mom Alone*, audio podcast, November 30, 2020, https://dontmomalone.com/2020/11/30/how-to-have-healthy-conflict-lynn-hoffman-ep-307.

6. Lisa-Jo Baker, "Healing Friendship Wounds," episode 159, *Don't Mom Alone*, audio podcast, April 3, 2017, https://dontmomalone.com/2017/04/03/healing-friendship-wounds-lisa-jo-baker-ep-159.

7. Brestin, *Friendships of Women*, 113.

8. Dr. John Townsend, "Setting Healthy Boundaries with Family," episode 250, *Don't Mom Alone*, audio podcast, June 3, 2019, https://dontmomalone.com/2019/06/03/setting-healthy-boundaries-with-family-dr-john-townsend-ep-250.

9. Townsend, "Setting Healthy Boundaries with Family."

10. Shundria Riddick, "Healing from Broken Friendships," episode 321, *Don't Mom Alone*, audio podcast, April 5, 2021, https://dontmomalone.com/2021/04/05/healing-from-broken-friendships-shundria-riddick-ep-321/.

11. Baker, "Healing Friendship Wounds."

12. Brestin, *Friendships of Women*, 120.

13. Lysa TerKeurst, Kay Wyma, and Courtney DeFeo, "Uninvited," episode 131, *Don't Mom Alone*, audio podcast, August 29, 2016, https://dontmomalone.com/2016/08/29/uninvited-lysa-terkeurst-kay-wyma-courtney-defeo-ep-131.

Chapter 7 All Working Moms

1. Dr. Emily W. King (@emilywkingphd), Instagram, March 23, 2020, https://www.instagram.com/p/B-Fs7n_HuiP.

2. Kat Armstrong, "Motherhood, Career, and Identity," episode 171, *Don't Mom Alone,* audio podcast, June 26, 2017, https://dontmomalone.com/2017/06/26/motherhood-career-identity-kat-armstrong-ep-171/.

3. Kendra Adachi, "Choose What Matters to You," episode 293, *Don't Mom Alone*, audio podcast, August 24, 2020, https://dontmomalone.com/2020/08/24/choose-what-matters-to-you-kendra-adachi-ep-293/.

4. Aubrie Norman, "When You Carry the Burden of Perfection," *Don't Mom Alone*, episode 284, May 4, 2020, https://dontmomalone.com/2020/05/04/when-you-carry-the-burden-of-perfection-aubrie-norman-ep-284/.

5. Jo Saxton, "Embracing the Mom You're Meant to Be," episode 283, *Don't Mom Alone*, audio podcast, April 27, 2020, https://dontmomalone.com/2020/04/27/embracing-the-mom-youre-meant-to-be-jo-saxton-ep-283.

6. Jeni B, "Rebuilding from an Abusive Marriage," episode 246, *Don't Mom Alone*, audio podcast, May 6, 2019, https://dontmomalone.com/2019/05/06/rebuilding-from-an-abusive-marriage-jeni-b-ep-246/.

Chapter 8 Keep the Candles Lit

1. Beth McCord, "The Enneagram, Marriage and the Gospel," episode 259, *Don't Mom Alone*, audio podcast, September 30, 2019, https://dontmomalone.com/2019/09/30/the-enneagram-marriage-and-the-gospel-beth-mccord-ep-259.

2. McCord, "Enneagram, Marriage and the Gospel."

3. *Brené Brown: The Call to Courage*, directed by Sandra Restrepo (Netflix, 2019).

4. Francie Winslow, "The Ripple Effect of Healthy Sexual Connection," episode 138, *Don't Mom Alone*, audio podcast, October 17, 2016, https://dontmomalone.com/2016/10/17/the-ripple-effect-of-healthy-sexual-connection-francie-winslow-ep-138.

5. Shauna Niequist, "Soulful Over Frantic," episode 127, *Don't Mom Alone*, audio podcast, August 1, 2016, https://dontmomalone.com/2016/08/01/soulful-over-frantic-shauna-niequist-ep-127.

6. Paul David Tripp, "Habits of a Healthy Marriage," episode 234, *Don't Mom Alone*, audio podcast, February 11, 2019, https://dontmomalone.com/2019/02/11/habits-of-a-healthy-marriage-paul-david-tripp-ep-234.

7. Beth Moore, "Grace According to Our Needs," episode 270, *Don't Mom Alone*, audio podcast, January 20, 2020, https://dontmomalone.com/2020/01/20/grace-according-to-our-needs-beth-moore-ep-270.

Chapter 9 Don't Make Me Angry

1. Thomas Aquinas, *Summa Theologica*, trans. Fathers of the Dominican Province (New York: Benziger Brothers, 1911–1925), II–II, q. 158.

2. Jeremy Safran and Leslie Greenberg, "Feeling, Thinking, and Acting: A Cognitive Framework for Psychotherapy Integration," *Journal of Cognitive Psychotherapy* 2 (1988): 109–31.

3. Scott Turansky and Joanne Miller, *Good and Angry: Exchanging Frustration for Character in You and Your Kids!* (Carol Stream, IL: Shaw, 2002), 17.

4. Amber Lia, "What Triggers Your Angry Reaction?," episode 108, *Don't Mom Alone*, audio podcast, February 15, 2016, https://dontmomalone.com/2016/02/15/what-triggers-your-angry-reaction-amber-lia-ep-108/.

5. Turansky and Miller, *Good and Angry*, 98–99.

6. Turansky and Miller, *Good and Angry*, 3.

7. Kirk Martin, "How to Stop Yelling, Lecturing, and Power Struggles," episode 62, *Don't Mom Alone*, audio podcast, March 2, 2015, https://dontmomalone.com/2015/03/02/stop-yelling-lecturing-power-struggles-today-kirk-martin-ep-62.

Chapter 10 Like Riding a Horse

1. Clay Clarkson, *Heartfelt Discipline: Following God's Path of Life to the Heart of Your Child*, 2nd ed. (Monument, CO: Whole Heart Press, 2012), 33.
2. Paul David Tripp, "Gospel Parenting," episode 176, *Don't Mom Alone*, audio podcast, September 11, 2017, https://dontmomalone.com/2017/09/11/gospel -parenting-paul-david-tripp-ep-176.
3. Tripp, "Gospel Parenting."
4. Jim and Lynne Jackson, *Discipline that Connects with Your Child's Heart: Building Faith, Wisdom, and Character in the Messes of Daily Life* (Minneapolis: Bethany, 2016), 27.
5. Jackson and Jackson, *Discipline that Connects with Your Child's Heart*, 33.
6. Karis Kimmel Murray, "Grace-Based Discipline," episode 150, *Don't Mom Alone*, audio podcast, January 30, 2017, https://dontmomalone.com/2017/01/30 /grace-based-discipline-Karis-Kimmel-Murray-ep-150.
7. Jeannie Cunnion, "Anchoring Our Kids' Lovability in Christ," episode 91, *Don't Mom Alone*, audio podcast, https://dontmomalone.com/2015/10/12/anchor ing-our-kids-lovability-in-christ-jeannie-cunnion-ep-91.
8. Murray, "Grace-Based Discipline."
9. Amy McCready, "How as Little as 20 Minutes a Day Can Change Your Whole Year," *Positive Parenting Solutions,* https://www.positiveparentingsolu tions.com/parenting/how-as-little-as-20-minutes-a-day-can-change-your-whole -year.
10. Tripp, "Gospel Parenting."
11. H. Clay Trumbull, *Hints on Child Training* (Eugene, OR: Great Expectations Book Company, 1999; originally published in 1891), 47.
12. Trumbull, *Hints on Child Training*, 49.

Chapter 11 Throw Away the Receipt

1. Alice, "Adopting Special Needs: Alice & Candace," episode 213, *Don't Mom Alone*, audio podcast, August 20, 2018, https://dontmomalone.com/2018 /08/20/adopting-special-needs-alice-candace-ep-213/.
2. Heather Zempel, *Amazed and Confused: When God's Actions Collide with Our Expectations* (Nashville: Thomas Nelson, 2014), 30.
3. Tricia Goyer, "An Interview with Tricia Goyer," episode 7, *Don't Mom Alone*, audio podcast, December 30, 2013, https://dontmomalone.com/2013/12 /30/an-interview-with-tricia-goyer-gcm-podcast-episode-7.
4. Sally Clarkson, *Seasons of a Mother's Heart,* 2nd ed. (Anderson, IN: Apologia, 2009), 136.
5. Clarkson, *Seasons of a Mother's Heart*, 139.
6. Ann Voskamp, "10 Point Manifesto of Joyful Parenting," https://annvos kamp.com/10-points-of-joyful-parenting-printable.
7. Phillips, "Listening to the Lord."
8. Sally Clarkson, "Loving Your 'Different' Child: Sally & Nathan Clarkson," episode 149, *Don't Mom Alone*, audio podcast, January 23, 2017, https://dontmom alone.com/2017/01/23/loving-your-different-child-sally-nathan-clarkson-ep-149/.

9. David Thomas, "The Art of Nurturing Boys," episode 119, *Don't Mom Alone*, audio podcast, May 9, 2016, https://dontmomalone.com/2016/05/09/the -art-of-nurturing-boys-david-thomas-ep-119/.

10. Lynne Jackson, "Helping Your Child with Sensory Processing Issues," episode 258, *Don't Mom Alone*, audio podcast, September 23, 2019, https://dont momalone.com/2019/09/23/helping-your-child-with-sensory-processing-issues -lynne-jackson-ep-258.

11. Charissa Fry, "The Window of Tolerance," episode 260, *Don't Mom Alone*, audio podcast, October 7, 2019, https://dontmomalone.com/2019/10/07/the-win dow-of-tolerance-charissa-fry-ep-260.

Chapter 12 Do Like I Do

1. Mary DeMuth, "Building the Family You Never Had," episode 156, *Don't Mom Alone*, audio podcast, March 13, 2017, https://dontmomalone.com/2017 /03/13/building-the-family-you-never-had-mary-demuth-ep-156/.

2. Dr. Kara Powell, "Build Lasting Faith in Your Kids," episode 290, *Don't Mom Alone*, audio podcast, June 15, 2020, https://dontmomalone.com/2020/06 /15/build-lasting-faith-in-your-kids-dr-kara-powell-ep-290.

3. Powell, "Build Lasting Faith in Your Kids."

4. Jen Wilkin, "Debunking Spiritual Leadership Myths," episode 128, *Don't Mom Alone*, audio podcast, August 8, 2016, https://dontmomalone.com/2016/08 /08/debunking-spiritual-leadership-myths-jen-wilkin-ep-128.

5. George Barna, *Revolutionary Parenting: What the Research Shows Really Works* (Carol Stream, IL: Tyndale Momentum, 2010), 30.

6. Barna, *Revolutionary Parenting*, 103.

7. Quoted in Susan Ratcliffe, *Concise Oxford Dictionary of Quotations* (Oxford: Oxford University Press, 2011), 389.

8. Jodie Berndt, "Praying the Scriptures," episode 194, *Don't Mom Alone*, audio podcast, February 19, 2018, https://dontmomalone.com/2018/02/19/praying -the-scriptures-jodie-berndt-ep-194.

9. Jodie Berndt, *Praying the Scriptures for Your Children: Discover How to Pray God's Will for Their Lives*, 20th anniversary ed. (2001; Grand Rapids: Zondervan, 2020), 21.

10. Caroline Boykin, *The Well-Versed Family: Raising Kids of Faith Through Scripture Memory* (Mustang, OK: Tate Publishing, 2007), 133–35.

11. Powell, "Build Lasting Faith in Your Kids."

12. Barna, *Revolutionary Parenting*, 106.

13. Paul David Tripp, "Opportunity vs. Disruption," episode 212, *Don't Mom Alone*, audio podcast, August 13, 2018, https://dontmomalone.com/2018/08/13 /opportunity-vs-disruption-paul-david-tripp-ep-212.

Also Available from
Heather MacFadyen

Find a curated list of *Don't Mom Alone*
episodes that are mentioned in each chapter.
Scan the QR code below with your smartphone or visit
https://dontmomalone.com/bookepisodes/

ABOUT

Heather MacFadyen

HEATHER MACFADYEN wrote online before Facebook existed. After years of blog entries, in 2013 she launched a trailblazing podcast called *God Centered Mom*. In 2018, the show rebranded to the *Don't Mom Alone* podcast. With over thirteen million downloads, Heather's weekly interviews have been listened to at least once in every country on the planet. When she's not recording conversations in her messy closet, she's driving in Dallas traffic, feeding four growing boy-men, or walking around the "hood" with her entrepreneurial husband, Bruce.

Connect with

Heather

dontmomalone.com

⊙ f @dontmomalone

A RESOURCEFUL COMMUNITY
FOR MOMS

DON'T
M○M
ALONE

PODCAST
WITH HEATHER MACFADYEN

TUNE IN WHEREVER YOU
GET YOUR PODCASTS